PRAISE FOR *YOU HAVE THE MAGIC*

"Haley is a masterful wordsmith who has the ability to help you access the hidden powers of your subconscious mind in the most relatable and accessible way I've ever experienced. This book is chock-full of tools and examples that will completely rewire your brain to not only see the best in life but also manifest it. Prepare to have your life changed."

—Kathrin Zenkina, manifestation expert
& CEO/founder of Manifestation Babe

"A transformative toolkit for anyone ready to rewrite their story, Haley Hoffman Smith's *You Have the Magic* combines evidence-based research, practical tools, and empowering inspiration in a fun, witty package to help readers break through the roadblocks holding them back."

—Mary Poffenroth, PhD, author of *Brave New You:*
Strategies, Tools, and Neurohacks to Live More Courageously Every Day

"A phenomenally empowering read! Backed by science and practical methodologies, Hoffman Smith teaches us how to manifest the life we've always dreamed of."

—Nina Purewal, internationally bestselling author of *Let That Sh*t Go*

"An electric blend of science and spirit, *You Have the Magic* offers a fresh, tangible approach to manifestation. Haley Hoffman Smith demystifies the subconscious, enabling readers to tap into their own limitless potential and transform their reality."

—Aliza Kelly, author of *This Is Your Destiny:*
Using Astrology to Manifest Your Best Life

"Haley Hoffman Smith masterfully blends inspiration with practicality in *You Have the Magic*. It's not just a book; it's a toolkit for transformation, written with warmth, humor, and wisdom that will resonate deeply with readers."

—Emma Mumford, leading manifestation expert
and bestselling author of *Positively Wealthy*

"Haley Hoffman Smith redefines what manifestation really means in *You Have the Magic*. Like Haley, I felt stuck in my early twenties until a chance manifestation workshop changed the course of my life. Marrying research with a relatable narrative voice, Haley shares science-backed tools that will empower and inspire. This genre-bending book is a must-read for anyone who wants to change the way they think, live, and feel."

—Sarah Levy, author of *Drinking Games: A Memoir*

YOU HAVE THE MAGIC

**Harness the Power
of Your Mind to
Transform Your Reality**

HALEY
HOFFMAN
SMITH

RUNNING PRESS
PHILADELPHIA

Running Press
Hachette Book Group
1290 Avenue of the Americas, New York, NY 10104
www.runningpress.com
@Running_Press

First Edition: May 2025

Published by Running Press, an imprint of Hachette Book Group, Inc. The Running Press name and logo are trademarks of Hachette Book Group, Inc.

The Hachette Speakers Bureau provides a wide range of authors for speaking events. To find out more, go to www.hachettespeakersbureau.com or email HachetteSpeakers@hbgusa.com.

Running Press books may be purchased in bulk for business, educational, or promotional use. For more information, please contact your local bookseller or the Hachette Book Group Special Markets Department at Special.Markets@hbgusa.com.

The publisher is not responsible for websites (or their content) that are not owned by the publisher.

Print book cover design by Jack Smyth
Print book interior design by Amanda Richmond

Library of Congress Cataloging-in-Publication Data
Names: Hoffman Smith, Haley, author.
Title: You have the magic : harness the power of your mind to transform your reality / Haley Hoffman Smith.
Description: First edition. | Philadelphia : Running Press, 2025. | Includes bibliographical references.
Identifiers: LCCN 2024041420 (print) | LCCN 2024041421 (ebook) | ISBN 9780762489213 (hardcover) | ISBN 9780762489237 (ebook)
Subjects: LCSH: Self-actualization (Psychology) | Emotional Freedom Techniques. | Self-help techniques.
Classification: LCC BF637.S4 H5886 2025 (print) | LCC BF637.S4 (ebook) | DDC 158.1—dc23/eng/20241227
LC record available at https://lccn.loc.gov/2024041420
LC ebook record available at https://lccn.loc.gov/2024041421

ISBNs: 978-0-7624-8921-3 (hardcover), 978-0-7624-8923-7 (ebook)

Printed in the United States of America

LSC-C

Printing 1, 2025

CONTENTS

INTRODUCTION

Golden sunlight poured through the cracks between the blinds, and I felt the warmth on my skin, eyes still closed. I took a moment, lingering in the velvety darkness behind my eyelids, taking in the sparkly newness that filled the air and energy around me.

My eyes slowly opened, and I took in the most delightful, half-blurred sight: a cute little studio apartment, scattered boxes and suitcases, and a half-inflated mattress underneath me. I leapt out of bed, yanked the blinds up, and scurried to the bathroom to put in my contacts. As the world came into full clarity (thanks, Acuvue), I faced myself in the mirror and saw a glow within me that I'd never seen before. A glow of promise. Evidence that something irrevocable had changed within me, that in a way, everything over the preceding months and years had been leading me to this moment. The cityscape and a sliver of the Hudson River reflected in the mirror behind me seemed to wink in the sunlight, and I felt completely and utterly alive.

This was the first morning in my first New York City apartment. I had finally arrived from my hometown in Colorado, ready to follow my long-held dreams. But more importantly, my surroundings—the entire apartment, *my* new apartment, with its floor-to-ceiling windows, sunbeams dancing across the hardwoods, white kitchen, and even that tiny sliver of the Hudson River—**formed the exact scene I had constructed in my mind's eye months prior.** It was uncanny, otherworldly. And the story of how I had arrived there was even more glorious than I could have fathomed.

Now, if you had shown this image to the version of me just one year or even six months prior, I would never have believed it could be real. It had been every type of impossible to me; a pipe dream that MAYBE I could have seen myself achieving in a decade if I was lucky. That version of me was living in my hometown, an unemployed college graduate who was capital-*M Miserable*. I had tried to take the leap to start my own business after bravely quitting my first postgrad job, and that leap ended up being more like a freefall. Without a parachute. Into a dark abyss of resistance, stagnation, procrastination, and compromised self-esteem.

We'll get into the gory details later, but the truth is, I am beyond grateful for my *looooong* swim in that swampy abyss because without it, I never would have discovered the tools that would one day take me to higher ground. I never would have addressed what was REALLY going on beneath the surface and taken steps to validate the dreams I'd had my entire life. Even the most trying and difficult times in our lives have the potential to be the soil in which our new beginnings sprout, if we choose to see their potential. Although part of me still cringes when I see photos from that time in *my* life, I also worship at the altar of that swampy year because it shaped the most amazing expansion, the blooming that would happen next.

Maybe you're feeling the same way right now: lost in the abyss. You can usually tell you're there when hope feels low and everything that could thrill you feels impossible, or like there's a block between you and it. Maybe it seems so easy for others, but never for you. Maybe you get really great ideas and bursts of energy at inopportune times like right before bed, and you promise you'll start on them tomorrow, only to feel like you picked up a backpack filled with twenty-seven dumbbells when the next day comes. Heavy. Icky. Stuck.

Maybe you've been wanting something for your life for *so* long, but it just hasn't been happening, and so now you're almost *expecting* discouragement. Maybe you get close every time, but always seem to fall short.

Put simply, maybe one part—or even *every* part—of your life has made you believe magic is only found in children's books about mystical realms. I get it.

I'm here to change that misconception.

To me, magic is not (necessarily) pulling bunnies out of hats or trailing pixie dust wherever you walk. It's how I like to think about the incredible energetic creative power we have to transform our lives when we clear the barriers in the way.

The truth is, this time next week, your life could look completely different. TOMORROW, your life could look completely different. Even a micro-shift in your energy can steer your life onto a whole new track. A life-changing idea that arrives out of the blue. A chance encounter with someone who opens a door for you (literally or metaphorically). A new way of viewing the world and your place in it. A shift in your belief that creates a shift in your external reality.

This book is many things, but at the core it is a handbook to tap into the magic that you have within you, and the magic that always surrounds you, and use it to *absolutely change your life.*

But I want to be clear. This book isn't just about fulfilling vision board items and manifesting them into your reality, like how I did with my New York City apartment. And it isn't about abstract, airy-fairy concepts, even if its concepts do feel pretty *magical.*

This book is rooted in neuroscience and the proven ways our brains actually control what shows up in our reality.

And my goal is to share this information in the most accessible, easy-to-understand way possible. You will grasp how your brain's neural pathways and your subconscious beliefs have shaped your life with incredible precision. This insight is so satisfying and illuminating that as you read, I bet you'll find yourself calculating your own subconscious breakthroughs all the time. (You may even help some click together for friends and family members, something I have way too much fun doing.)

The Subconscious Breakthrough Formula presented in this book is basically a new lens through which you'll learn to see the world—one that will clear up so many mysteries. Like a pattern emerging out of the fog. And it's my promise to you that you'll never see the world—or yourself—in the same way after reading it and following the exercises.

I know something led you to this book. You've suspected for a long time—your whole life, maybe—that there is more available to you than what meets the eye. Maybe you, too, tried wishing on stars and fireflies growing up, or you've had awe-inspiring moments that made you suspect life has wonderful secrets in store for you. Or maybe you've just seen miracles happen for others, and curiosity got the best of you. Maybe this is your last-ditch effort at believing in something beyond, or maybe it's an exciting next step of a journey that's already been so expansive and fulfilling.

Whatever brought you here is magic, too. We are guided to what we need at the right time. When something piques our curiosity, it's our soul saying, *"Yes! THAT! That's what I need for the next step."* As you navigate the book, you'll feel your life begin to change because your awareness has changed. You'll see how what you focus on and what you do with your energy has an immediate and undeniable effect on your reality. You'll uncover deeper layers within you than ever before, creating a self-awareness that feels like coming home to yourself. And you'll learn all the tools you need to radically shift everything.

I promise, if I could be totally stuck with no motivation, wasting my days snacking on granola on the couch and scrolling social media in my hometown, then suddenly skyrocket to my dream apartment, my dream city, and the success and career fulfillment I'd always dreamed of within a *year* . . . you can, too. But you don't just have to take it from me. This book is full of stories from my coaching clients and those in my community who have experienced the same radical shifts in their own lives, in their own ways. They had their own subconscious breakthroughs with their own unique beliefs, memories, and self-concepts. And it helped each of them catapult into their own custom version of THEIR highest success and fulfillment.

In this book, you'll learn the exact steps and processes that I took and that I now teach in my Dreamaway membership community. The truth is, I stumbled into this work *because* it works. I started seeing such incredible shifts and changes, and when people would ask me how it was all happening, the answer was that I'd started subconscious breakthrough work utilizing a modality called EFT (Emotional Freedom Technique) Tapping to release emotional blockages and limiting beliefs. I was actively rewiring my brain—and as within, so without. The internal shifts to my self-concept and what I believed was possible for myself resulted in rapid consequent changes in my external reality.

In this book, you'll learn what a subconscious breakthrough is, how to give yourself one, and how to play detective to understand *why* you've been stuck or you're not yet where you want to be in your life. This, to me, is the most exciting part. I call these answers "No wonder!"s because once you identify the core memory or belief behind a repeated pattern or stuckness, it doesn't seem so random anymore. And then you know how to release it and step into a more empowering story and self-concept.

You'll then learn about EFT Tapping in its entirety: the exact technique I teach, which has resulted in massive shifts and changes for thousands of people, helping them get significant raises at work, unlock dream opportunities, meet their soulmates, start their businesses, scale on social media, and just generally enjoy life more. I'll show you how to use the process on yourself to achieve shifts in real time.

Mindset is a journey. Before we get into the subconscious and tapping magic, you'll first learn how much your beliefs, thoughts, expectations, and daily actions create the sum total of your life experience. You'll learn how to utilize visualization to create new experiences. You'll learn hacks for rewiring your mind while you sleep at night and the best way to vision board. You'll expand your innate power in every chapter, truly understand how much magic is already within you, and wake it up from its dormant state so you can experience real-life miracles.

And then, of course, there's the magic beyond us. This book will also help you deepen your partnership with the Universe, Source, God—whatever you want to call it, whatever you believe in. Whatever your relationship with your faith is, goose bumps are inbound. When we connect to something beyond us and realize we are constantly receiving signs and guidance, we open to the truth that EVERYTHING is guiding our highest evolution.

I'm so glad you're here. Wherever you currently are in life, however you're currently feeling, this book will create energetic ripple effects throughout your existence. You'll be able to point back one day and say, "That? That's where *everything* changed for me." That one day might even be tomorrow.

Reconnecting—or connecting for the first time—with the part of you that is aware of your magical gift to transform your entire life will do just that.

Because maybe, just maybe ...

---

you have always been the magic.

AUTHOR'S NOTE ON SAFETY

The techniques presented in this book are supported by phenomenally exciting research for their efficacy. Although still being researched, EFT Tapping in particular has a growing body of studies and testimonials behind it. That said, some investigations into memories that involve significant trauma require the utmost care, and in these cases, I would advise that readers follow the techniques presented in part 2 only while working one-on-one with a licensed therapist or mental health professional.

The techniques presented in this book are not a substitute for therapy or any form of counseling, and they should not be used to contend with significant trauma. The intention of *You Have the Magic* is to help you discover and release subconscious blocks to uplevel in many areas of your life, but this is not a book written for or about trauma or psychotherapy. Many licensed therapists utilize EFT Tapping and other forms of subconscious discovery, and I wholeheartedly recommend booking sessions with them if you suspect that any content in this book or in your journaling might lead to emotionally challenging depths.

You are supported, and great peace awaits you, no matter which way you choose to utilize this powerful process and modality.

PART 1

YOU ARE THE MAGIC

CHAPTER 1

TODAY IS OPEN
TO INTERPRETATION

Today could be the day that changes your life forever.

Seriously—today! Even with all its perceived inadequacies: your laundry list of to-dos, off weather, being out of coffee grounds again (a big no-no in my household of one). In fact, in my experience, it's usually those *blah* days that end up being some of the most pivotal of my life . . . because unfortunately, we're seldom inspired to change our entire lives when we're on a tropical summer vacation. But in the dead of winter (metaphorically or literally), when morale is low and a shakeup feels most *needed*—that's when you find the fertile soil for some major life changes.

During one such winter, when I was in college, I was in the midst of a certifiably blah slump. It was about that time when everyone was lining up summer internships and zeroing in on their postgrad careers, and I had absolutely no direction, no sense of how to move forward. None of the available options appealed to me. I had recently experienced a dramatic epiphany: I wanted to be a revered global talk show host superstar. I wanted to have my own platform, and also get more involved in entrepreneurship, and basically be the boss of my life while sharing juicy information with a wide audience all day. How hard could it be?

Unfortunately, there's no internship to become a talk show host superstar (at least that I am aware of, but let me know if you hear of one), so I was floundering, desperate to find something that could *maybe* put me on the right track. I even interviewed with a news station in my hometown and asked on the phone, "But are there any opportunities for *me* to become the news anchor?" Which—why would that even happen? A college girl waltzes in just for the summer and suddenly becomes an overnight sensation, reporting on the weather and local crime? I was a *little* off base, but bless my heart for trying.

What the heck was I going to do after I graduated if I couldn't even find a summer internship opportunity that felt expansive to me? I resigned myself to a plan in which I'd find a summer job for some cash and figure the rest out later. The road ahead was foggy, and my heart was in deep despair over it. Throw in some dark, cold Rhode Island winter weather, and you have yourself the perfect set design for this scene in the movie of my life.

The days started to blur together, each feeling darker and colder than the last. I began to spend more time in my dorm room, huddled with a big gallon box of Goldfish, binge-watching Netflix (and feeling jealous of the Netflix stars—how did *they* get to where they were?), becoming increasingly blah and losing my motivation and my sparkle. I didn't want to go do anything fun, and my energy levels were constantly at zero. I was stuck. And I had good reason to be! It felt like a huge inconvenience to dream as big as I was dreaming.

One day, out of desperation and a need for a major distraction on my long, bitingly cold walks to class, I downloaded some mindset audiobooks on abundance and manifesting: specifically, how to manifest money. Because who doesn't like money? I figured if I could generate wealth, I could forge some of my own epic opportunities, like building a studio and hiring a film crew for my own talk show. This audiobook felt like a good place to start.

As I started listening, something began to shift within me. The books talked so much about the power of MINDSET and ENERGY—a real "your entire life is up to you, and you can make ANYTHING happen" knockout message that rattled me and broke open my horizons.

It was minor at first (it always is), but I noticed that as I was consuming this content, a snowball effect started to occur, and the mental shift within me grew more powerful. I was taking it all to heart. If my situation was really just up to my mindset and my energy, then I realized I'd better get started! Before I began down this manifesting-book road, all my thoughts had been centered on ideas like *woe is me, my dreams will never come true,* and *everything is cold,* and that mindset was just making everything worse. It becomes increasingly easy to keep thinking negatively when you're already thinking negatively, and I had perfected that downward spiral. But this new content I was consuming was so positive, and so focused on the idea *opportunity is out there!,* that the wheels in my brain started turning in the opposite direction. Maybe all was not lost. Maybe I just wasn't looking in the right places.

As I started expanding my worldview to think about more and more possibilities, a new "spiral" started to happen—an upward one. The books shared so many stories and anecdotes of others who had totally transformed their lives, manifested their dream careers or homes or cars, and landed their dream clients by shifting their perspective and energy—and I was lapping it all up like a vanilla cappuccino. I couldn't stop.

I listened while standing in the omelet line at the dining hall, in my lecture halls 'til the second my professors began class, and while pacing my dorm room. I felt this excitement start to grow within me. And I held tightly to it, too, not letting anything touch it. Within just a few days of this, my laptop decided to fizzle out and stop working. But I was determined not to react with the familiar downward mindset spiral to this unpleasant circumstance, even though I had a paper due that week and it would have been a great opportunity to grit my teeth, roll my eyes, and yell at the sky. Armed with my new attitude, I refused!

I grabbed my kaput laptop and marched to the student center to get some tech help, and as I stepped outside, I was immediately pelted with a nice, mushy, frigid snow-rain mixture unique to those Rhode Island winters. I was quickly soaked head to toe and began Slip-'N-Sliding down the campus sidewalks as I hiked toward laptop resuscitation. But despite all of that, my mind wasn't pulled into the pessimistic place it would have been a few weeks earlier. Now, I was DETERMINED not to let these setbacks shake my mood.

"I'm grateful that I *can* go to a student center for help!" I thought, refusing to acknowledge the puddle I'd just stepped in, soaking my entire right foot.

"I'm grateful that I even *have* a laptop!" I mentally recited, smiling intentionally and choosing to be unfazed by the passerby's umbrella that almost took my eye out.

Sure enough, I reached my destination, and my computer was fixed within a few days. My foot thawed. Everything worked out okay. And since I had to reset my password for my email when I logged on to the loaner computer they gave me in the meantime, I made the new password "Gratitude" with a series of my favorite numbers as a reminder to be grateful in all circumstances.

Suddenly, the next few days started to sparkle with opportunity and an extra glow because I was thinking differently and more aware of magic around me. I started wearing bright lipstick for fun and thinking about ideas for programs I could launch on campus that *would* light me up. I'm on the introverted side, but I started to put myself out there and network with other students and stay longer after the end of events and class to talk to people. And I found something incredible: the more I moved in one direction, the more that surge of energy would carry me forward and open up new doors. The more life sparkled, the more those sparkles would grow and grow.

At this point in my life, I had already taken stabs at some entrepreneurial ventures. The summer after my freshman year of college, I had started a global nonprofit called Lit Without Limits, which donated books and an accompanying curriculum to girls around the world in mentoring groups. I had scaled the ambassador program for this nonprofit to nearly one hundred global individuals on social media at one point. I knew from this work how much I loved forging my own path, being a leader, and making a difference. Now I was ready to go all in and lean on that experience as I kept looking through my new glasses with the prescription: "Even MORE opportunity is out there, and things WILL keep getting better and better."

The thing about that mindset is it's absolutely true, and we never know just HOW the story will unfold. But what IS important is to notice what comes up as we implement the mindset and see the world through a new lens, and to follow the divine winks . . .

Opportunity, Indeed

Like magic, within these life-altering few weeks, I heard about an upcoming seminar called "How to Create Your Life." Was this just what the doctor ordered, or WHAT? I planned my day around attending, ready to get the inside scoop on how to become a Talk Show Superstar and bring my big life vision to fruition.

The seminar was hosted by J. Douglas Bate, coauthor of *The Power of Strategy Innovation*, and because like attracts like, I quickly realized it shared a lot of the key themes I'd been studying in my self-proclaimed Magic Audiobook University. It was everything I needed to hear. I realized more than ever before that the big vision I had for my life was what I wanted more than ANYTHING, and even though I had absolutely no idea on how to get there, I was going to do whatever it took to make it happen.

One main message he shared in the seminar was the "genius of the AND." In other words, instead of always needing to choose just ONE thing to go after, we should always believe there is more out there. We need this out-of-the-box thinking to change our paradigm.

I ended up emailing him after the seminar, wondering if I could get his take. Here's a real transcript of part of the email:

> I always imagined that I would attend law school or business school postgrad—still viable and attractive considerations. But, as your talk clarified for me, what I really want to do with my life is . . . to be in front of the camera.
>
> So the heart of my dilemma is this: how do you advise someone whose electrifying vision is so far from the life they have been working towards? I suppose I felt as though climbing the mountains of my women empowerment efforts and my efforts at an Ivy League institution were leading to a precipice—I did not expect it to be something so different, and a question within itself. It admittedly sparks some regret, and absolutely some panic!

Doug kindly replied and offered to meet with me. He shared with me advice that would become so helpful on my journey: "Keep that energy alive by imagining the future you want in the next chapter of your life, which will allow you to see opportunities everywhere," he told me. That I did.

In the subsequent weeks, I kept following those opportunities. An impromptu coffee with a friend from the campus entrepreneurship program ended with an introduction to a Facebook community of thousands of entrepreneurs, and a few posts and comments in that group led to more phone calls and introductions. With all these energizing links, I was spending much less time watching Netflix, and much more time in the buzz of potential and connection.

As a result of all these shifts and happenings, even though the only things I'd changed were my outlook and what I was saying "yes" to, life started to look incredibly different. Providence, Rhode Island, where I was living and studying at Brown, is far from a big city, but one of the opportunities posted in this entrepreneurship group happened to be for a *paid* gig speaking on a Young Entrepreneurs panel in . . . you guessed it, Providence! And the panel was scheduled to happen in just a few weeks! What "lucky" timing. (Wink, wink.)

I applied and was accepted, and I became fast friends with the other panelists on the day of the speaking engagement. The other panelists inspired me so much; they were all renowned entrepreneurs and had such interesting perspectives, book recommendations, and ways of seeing the world. We all attended a private dinner afterward prepared by Johnson & Wales culinary students, and we laughed for hours, sharing stories and inspiration.

Suddenly, it dawned on me how much I could feel my horizons broadening. It was easier to think bigger, especially getting to talk with and learn from other entrepreneurs my age—I was making friends with individuals who inspired me, who I'd been led to on this brand-new wave of energy! *And* I made a few hundred dollars from the gig—my first time ever getting paid to speak! Then, I was invited to speak at the Brown Women in Business club the following week. Was I . . . becoming a renowned global talk show superstar? Not quite, but I certainly felt like I was on the right track, and I was falling in love with the rush of it all: seeing the progress, feeling the excitement, and noticing how my external reality was mirroring these internal shifts. It was such a perfect set of domino circumstances that I couldn't believe were falling for me.

And it's just that: dominoes. If we could rewind my life backwards from the moment I got on that stage for that panel, we'd see that the little push that made the first domino fall was the change in my perception and mood just a short time prior. These are the points where life splits off into numerous potential paths branching out in front of us. We can stay where we are and continue to do and feel the same things, and therefore attract more of what we have been attracting. OR we can start to make different choices and show up differently, and *then* we're cooking with heat. Then entirely new circumstances reveal themselves, and they lead us in different directions.

It reminds me of the Steve Jobs quote "You can't connect the dots looking forward, only looking back." When you look back one day, you'll see that the whole new path really did start with one small decision. You made a different choice, or showed up in a different way, and suddenly you realized you veered from the path you were on, onto a whole new path that led you to an entirely new location, so far away from where you could've been had you never made the change.

The more you continue to make new choices, each toppling domino sets off the next, leading you somewhere new and different again . . . and again . . . and yet again. And it can start with a *single day*. And that day doesn't have to be the perfect day, or one you preplan for. That day can be today, as of this exact moment.

Remember that entrepreneurship community I was introduced to? That introduction was just the beginning of a larger adventure—and it ended up leading to *so* much more than just that one first paid speaking gig. In fact, it ended up shaping *my entire career to date*. But we'll get to that later. I'll leave you on this juicy cliff-hanger so you have to keep reading this book, and then you'll have no choice but to let me help you change your life.

What is most important for you to know as we begin is how much today matters, and that a single choice or a shift in mood can get you into a drastically different place from where you started. And as magical as that sounds, it's actually backed by neuroscience.

The Neuroscience of
Changing Your Life—Right NOW

None of us experience reality the same way. There are millions of bits of information and stimuli being thrown at us at any given moment—quite literally about eleven million bits per second, as I learned from an NPR interview with behavioral and data scientist Pragya Agarwal. And guess how many your conscious mind can process? A whopping forty to fifty of those bits. Which, according to my math, on the generous side, means your brain can process only about 0.0004 percent of what's actually happening. To really drive this home, that's THREE zeroes on the other side of the decimal point. That's not hyperbole; that's cold hard science, baby.

Let's play a game to try to understand *just* how significant this is. Take in the scene around you right now, wherever you are. How many things in the room around you are shiny? Purple? Fuzzy? What is the temperature? If you're in a public place, how many people around you are wearing something patterned? How many clouds are in the sky? What sounds are gently buzzing in the background, whether it's the whir of your air conditioner or the steady stream of cars whizzing by on the road outside?

You weren't focused on those details before I asked this question, because you didn't *need* to be. Those details weren't relevant until I made them relevant by asking you to look for them. But that didn't mean they weren't around you. We move through the world and our lives missing a LOT of details, and we're okay with that, because we aren't focused on what we're missing! We're seeing what we *are* looking for. It's like if you're in a coffee shop and I call you and ask you to check the menu to see if they have matcha. Then, after you see it on the menu and tell me that yes, they do, I ask if you happened to see if they also had hot chocolate. You probably didn't see that option because you weren't looking for it, but your eyes still skimmed over it. It was a bit of information or external stimuli that you didn't perceive or integrate, even though it was right in front of you.

This is important because we see only what we are focused on or looking for. Everything else is muted in the background. If you're sitting and working at a crowded coffee shop, you're not listening to people ordering, even if you *could* tune in and listen to see what's popular these days. And we've all found ourselves in the hyperfocus of a task or a really good book when someone has been trying to get our attention. It takes them several attempts to pull us out of what we were focusing on, and we need them to repeat what they just said. When we zoom out and think about this in the context of whether we're focusing on, the good, bad, lucky, unlucky, full of opportunity, or "everything is dreary," it becomes clear WHY we get stuck in certain ways of seeing the world and our place in it. This becomes our "story" if we hold on to the point of focus for too long.

Now, you don't need to change your entire story today, nor am I asking you to—we can take this slow. But you *will* change your story over the course of this book. (Technically, you *could* do it all in one day, depending on your caffeine intake—but go at your own pace!)

For today, it can truly start with the little details and opening your eyes to what else is around you that you hadn't focused on before. Your assignment for the next few days, beginning right now: look for OPPORTUNITY.

I always think about the bulletin board of postings over the cream and sugar counter at a coffee shop. Imagine that after our phone call about matcha, when you were topping off your coffee with cream or grabbing a straw, your dream opportunity was actually right in front of your eyes on that bulletin board! "Chef wanted" or "Community theater hosting auditions." If you aren't actively thinking that opportunities for experiences you want are out there, you *will* miss that, even if it's staring you in the face. The Universe can deliver us blessings only if we're open to receiving them. Or maybe the Universe has nothing to do with this for you, and I'll just remind you that you're currently perceiving only forty to fifty bits of information per second out of the eleven million bits that are around you. If you aren't actively thinking about the opportunities you want, chances are you will completely miss any lead in your field of vision. And "chances" is an understatement there!

What if, all along, everything has been conspiring to help you get to exactly where your heart and soul want to go? But you've had blinders up, believing it's impossible or extremely hard? Your belief that it couldn't ever be that easy is *exactly* what you'll experience. I'm imagining you staring out a window with a forlorn look on your face, thinking, "Why can't I just get one little breadcrumb to lead me toward my dream opportunity?" when it's jumping up and down like a squirrel in front of the window, yelling, "I'm right here! Right here!"

This isn't your fault. It's all because of the brain's reticular activating system (RAS). The RAS helps us see what we've been thinking about and what we believe—and ONLY what we've been thinking about and what we believe. Want a new yellow Jeep? You'll suddenly see them everywhere, causing you to think for sure that everyone and their mother also wanted a yellow Jeep, and maybe you should select a more unique vehicle as your dream car. This is the RAS at work. As the gurus say, "What we focus on expands."

This, by the way, is also the reason that you believe there are so many people just like you in your chosen profession or who do your style of art. I talk to people all the time who say something like, "I really want to be a horseback riding instructor but there are just *so* many out there, the industry is too crowded and oversaturated!" Meanwhile, I'm raising an eyebrow because I've never met a horseback riding instructor in my entire life. My RAS has not been primed for that. (But good to know just in case one of my friends decides to take up horseback riding and needs an instructor.) The field isn't saturated to *me* at all. Different thoughts and experiences, different RAS filter, different evidence in our external realities.

It's the same with opportunities, connections, classes, and more. I always say that we experience what we believe. What we believe is not necessarily *true*—but what we believe *makes* it true *for us*. The reticular activating system has a "confirmation bias." Not only does it look for what we're already focused on, but it also wants to find further confirmation of what it already believes. This means you are significantly more inclined to see evidence of what you believe than evidence of a new idea you hadn't considered before! No wonder it's so hard to change our minds.

For example, I originally believed it would be a total shot in the dark to find career opportunities related to my "pipe dream" of becoming a Talk Show Superstar. I *believed* it was a pipe dream, which is a highly discouraging term to begin with. But as my belief started to shift and I let the lightin, I opened myself up to believing that maybe, just maybe, opportunity could be right under my nose . . . and there it was, every single time. Right on schedule. Right where I looked.

So as I began to look for more opportunities during that fateful year that changed my path, I found them! They weren't going to knock on my door until I sought them out, or at least started to think about them more. But they were *there*. The slight adjustment in my mindset created a corresponding change in my reality, in the same way that asking you to focus on the sounds around you created a change in your *experience* of reality in the present moment. The sounds were always there, but highlighting them through your focus and attention changed what you perceived.

Experience is subjective. Two people can be in the exact same environment and experience things completely differently. Imagine two people are on the same long-haul flight. They're in the same row of the plane. They're both in the window seats at opposite windows.

But despite the same environment, they could have two wildly different experiences based on what they're thinking about and focused on. To one of them, this flight is the worst experience ever. They feel cramped. The airplane food is disgusting. They forgot their headphones and had to pay for a set and one ear has static. None of the movie options appeal to them. They drank too much coffee during their layover and can't fall asleep.

But to the other person, this flight is one of their all-time coolest experiences. They're traveling long-haul for their first time ever, so a sense of adventure is in the air. They can't believe just how many movies the plane is offering—however will there be enough time to binge them all?! Oh, wait, they forgot their headphones, too. But they don't need them—they can't stop looking out the window and watching the vibrant colors of the sun setting as they soar through the sky, inspiring them to pull out their journal and get to writing. They decide to go a little wild and order two different types of drinks, because *abundance, baby!* And they fall asleep feeling so happy and excited, grateful for the adventure and the miracle of a plane to take them to their destination.

It's the exact same environment. Different points of focus. Different thought processes. Very, very different experiences as a result.

This gets really juicy when we think about a single day of our lives and how many different versions of that same day we could have based on what we're choosing to do, focus on, and think about. All it takes is a few minutes to shift gears and directions. Oftentimes, if we don't make the effort to make that shift, we also carry forward yesterday's thoughts, feelings, and focus points into today. And so on.

Today Lived in Two Very Different Ways

Let's play a little game of contrast. This will require some hypotheticals and is a bit extreme, but I simply mean to illustrate the number of ways you could live this very same next twelve hours of your life.

Imagine this as our first scenario: You spend tonight doing some good ol' fashioned Instagram stalking, selectively targeting your ex-partner, ex-friends, and maybe someone else who really ruined your life once. You bathe in their energy as you do this. Maybe you see something WILD, like breaking news *siren emoji*—your ex just got engaged—so you send a screenshot to your bestie and it sparks a long dramatic conversation, revisiting the worst parts of your relationship and how INTERESTING it is that they're now engaged, considering they were so non-committal to you.

Ding! Ding! Ding! Your thoughts and focus have homed in on a potent subject, and you're feeling all the emotions associated with that: Frustration. Anger. Jealousy. Residual heartbreak. The more you're in it, the harder it is to get out of it, because it feels so good in that moment to remember even more details or start another deep-dive stalking moment on their fiancée's cousin's charity's Facebook page and see what you can dig up from March 2017. Your mind has been ACTIVATED.

Then, let's say you chase that bitter pill down by watching a real thriller of a show to "get your mind off of it." (AKA, you didn't find anything on their fiancée's cousin's charity's Facebook page, believe it or not.) And this thriller has the works: high stakes, tearjerkers, and wild cliff-hangers that keep you pressing "next episode, please" until you end up going to sleep way past your self-proclaimed "latest bedtime." All night, your mind swirls with creative dreams involving your ex, their new fiancée, and a loose plotline resembling the TV show's scandal. You wake up still exhausted, with an activated nervous system, in one of your worst moods ever.

Recipe for an interesting day, don't you think? Moving forward through the morning, everything just feels like it's going wrong . . . because that's exactly where your mind is. You're still having imaginary arguments in your head with your ex, or your activated state has you already stressed out and cursing the day's workload or to-do list. Your mind is so overloaded that you forget to actually put coffee grounds in your coffee machine, so you end up with a nice pot of hot water when you're already late getting out the door. You can't find your darn other sock. Traffic seems worse than usual. Your phone charger isn't working. Everything is irritating you, and the day just seems to get worse, and worse, and worse...

Okay, let's change the channel away from that wild plummet downhill and try on a different perspective. Let's erase that hypothetical and reverse back to the start. Imagine that it's the SAME night. It's the same day of the week, the same date, the same weather, the same astrological influences, you've had the exact same series of happenings in your life up to this point. But you make a *different* choice.

Instead of going down a social media stalking rabbit hole, you do something lovely and productive like going by the grocery store and picking up some fresh foods to prepare a healthy dinner. Or you go for a run. Or hit the sauna. Or have a self-care night and listen to a great podcast about a topic that makes you happy. Or update your vision board (psst . . . at the end of this book you'll find a recipe for vision board–making that will rock your socks). Or you lose yourself in a romance novel, or call a friend and laugh for hours about funny, happy memories. Or you even really dial it up a notch and fall in love with your creative flow, finally working on an outline for the novel idea you've had forever or researching somewhere you really hope to visit.

And as you're bathing in THAT good energy, you may feel inclined to tidy up your space for the next day, and you put on some calming music.

You kick back and watch something comedic or inspirational with a nice face mask on. You close your eyes for just five minutes and picture something on your vision board. Really, doing ANY of these—even for *just five minutes*—will shift your energy so enormously, that the SAME NEXT MORNING will be experienced completely differently. You'll sleep better, and wake up feeling refreshed, hopeful, and in a better state of mind than the alternative. Traffic doesn't bother you because you're bopping to one of your favorite songs or intently listening to a good audiobook. You're less likely to forget your coffee grounds when making your morning coffee with your clear head, but if you do, it's cause for laughter and a funny text to a friend—and then what an amazing opportunity for a swing by your favorite coffee shop for a midweek treat. A shared smile with the barista boosts your spirits a little more. Maybe you even get a free coffee with all that abundant energy! You giggle at a meme on your phone and then send it to a few friends, sharing the laughter and high spirits. A brilliant idea pops into your head. The sun feels extra magical, with warm, golden sunbeams dancing on your shoulders as you walk to your car. Mmmm. Now that sounds nice.

You can turn your day around *right now*, simply by changing your energy, which starts by changing your actions and your point of focus. If I told you to close your eyes and think about something that really annoys you, you'd feel a visceral reaction of annoyance and agitation. Jaw clenches, heart races.

But if I told you to close your eyes right now and think of the cutest puppy you've ever seen, your favorite vacation you've ever been on, or the person you love most in the world, you'd have a very different visceral reaction. Everything loosens. Joy perks up in your chest. And that would attract more of the same. Feel joy? Get more of it. I think that's a pretty good deal.

What do we want? The good stuff! How do we get it? Moving our point of attraction by changing what we're doing and what we're focusing on.

This is not at all to say the secret of your life's great happiness and fulfillment is simply in thinking about puppies, although that would be epic and is worth a shot, and I must say it has worked for me on a number of occasions. And it's also not to say that life is about bypassing anything that's frustrating, hard, or annoying—in fact, we want to work WITH those moments to rewire our subconscious minds and change our lives, which we'll get into in depth later in this book. This is simply one piece of a much bigger puzzle. Understanding your own micro actions—the smaller choices you can make at a moment's notice—and how they have a real effect on your mood, and therefore your life, puts the power back into your hands to live a very different experience. And the more you do that consistently over time, the more the game changes, and your life changes.

I like to say that manifestation is really a game of manipulating the energies at your disposal. You are always surrounded by ENERGY and energy alone. Everything around you can be reduced down to atoms, and atoms are 99.9999999999999 percent empty space. Once again, I'm not adding a hyperbolic effect with all those digits. There are THIRTEEN 9s after that decimal point—cold, hard science once again, baby. And it's almost all empty space. Which, once again, means everything around you—including you—is MOSTLY ENERGY.

Something else that's energetic? Your emotions. And since it's all energy, your emotions are simultaneously responding to and influencing everything in your entire life experience. In this example of the two vastly different ways to spend one evening and the following morning, there was a certain amount of energy at your disposal. You had the evening, the free time, and the mental capacity. You manipulate this energy by carefully choosing what you do with it: what you think about, focus on, and what you set into motion.

You can think of your available energy right now as potential: what you choose to do with it from here will affect the next stream of energy that comes into your life, which means that at any given moment, you have TREMENDOUS power. Every moment is the first moment of the rest of your life. Including this one. Really soak in that power and feel the awesome potential and responsibility of that statement. Right now could be the moment you change everything simply by changing what you're focusing on and thinking about.

How do you know you're moving in the right direction? It's the one that feels best to you. Not necessarily the one that sounds the easiest or seems like the path of least resistance, because sometimes doomscrolling on social media or pushing off querying literary agents to tomorrow *again* sounds tantalizing. The one that *feels the best*, like a warm and fuzzy surge of power through your being. If you feel excited and energized by thinking about your new business idea or a weekend plan, that's confirmation. If you feel excited and energized when you imagine how you'll feel *after* taking this action, that's confirmation. It doesn't need to be your biggest leap ever; sometimes the smallest baby step of excitement is all that's required. Steps beyond that will reveal themselves. As these baby steps are repeated over time, and you continue to make choices in alignment with the energy of possibility and excitement, that's when everything starts to change. To prove this, let's think about how you got to where you currently are.

Habitual Thought

The thoughts you think aren't random. In fact, in starting this total life overhaul, you're going to be coming up against thoughts you've thought *habitually*. What are the most common thoughts you think about yourself, your job, your relationships, and your world?

I love journaling, and I've filled this book with little challenges or exercises that ask you to journal a bit, too. May the journey of self-discovery begin! You can write your answers in any way you'd like. Grab a journal, use the Notes app on your phone, type them out on your laptop—I just recommend you put your answers somewhere you can easily revisit them, so the back of that grocery store receipt might not be your best bet, unless you snap a picture of your answers afterward for safekeeping. We'll reflect on your answers throughout your subconscious breakthrough process.

Let's get to it. You can home in on what your most common thoughts are by writing a few statements for each area of your life. These statements are your current "truths"—they're reflections of what you believe and what you have been experiencing. Practice self-compassion as you write these out—we're just digging around to see what's happening "behind the scenes"!

For each of the following areas of your life, write down three to five statements about what you commonly experience and believe. It's okay if they're general. Whatever comes to mind will work—there's no way to "do this wrong," and we can learn a lot about ourselves from just seeing the first few statements that come to mind. And I challenge you to be as blunt and honest with yourself as possible. No one else will see this but you.

1. Your career
2. Your friendships

3. Your romantic relationship(s)
4. Your finances
5. Your family
6. Your health
7. Your habits
8. Your creativity
9. Your relationship with yourself
10. Your luck

To give you an idea, your statements could look like this for friendships:

1. I have a few really good friends who I can count on for anything—they're my lifers!
2. I've never had a big friend group and don't think I'd like it.
3. I often feel like I'm the most ambitious in my friend group.
4. My friends look to me for advice and it feels validating.

Or, like this for finances:

1. I've reached a comfortable salary and I'm proud of myself for that!
2. It feels difficult or impossible to imagine making more money. How could that even happen? My salary is my salary.
3. I feel so much safer when I save most of what I make.
4. I believe I can set my future self up for success by investing, and that's why I'm reading some beginner investment books.

Or, like this for a relationship with yourself:

1. I like to journal, and that helps me vent and process.
2. I seldom understand my really deep emotions.
3. I tend to be hard on myself when I don't perform my best.
4. I have great self-care nights when I need them.

Once you've written down three to five statements for each, I want you to go back and challenge yourself to write at least *five more statements*. These can be the same statements written in a different way, deeper dives, thoughts that felt too small or insignificant (no such thing) the first go-round, or anything that comes up. The reason I'm challenging you to do this is because we all have a "buffer" in our minds between the conscious and the subconscious. When we are challenged to keep coming up with more ideas, epiphanies, conclusions, or thoughts, we push past the first ones that come to mind (which are the ones swimming in our conscious mind) and start to tap into what's going on in the subconscious mind. This is going to be a key theme in rewriting your entire life, so this is a great place to begin.

Once this is complete, amazing! Now you have a picture of what's going on in the major facets of your life that directly reflects your beliefs. Did any of the answers surprise you—especially as you pushed past that initial buffer?

These main stories and beliefs in each area of your life have been constructed because of what has happened to date and what you've observed from others.

Imagine that someone has habitually thought that they're unlucky. Perhaps it's a belief system they adopted from their parents. "Unlucky things happen to me ALL THE TIME," they say, or the classic "That's just my luck."

Every time we think about something, our brain fires a neuron down the neural pathway of that thought. The more we think about something, the thicker the neural pathway becomes. And because our brains are energy efficient, the thicker the neural pathway becomes, the more likely it is that we will think that thought again. And again.

To explain this, imagine you're in your car and there are two ways to the same destination. One way is on a major highway that's paved and is a straight shot right to where you want to go. The other is a random backwoods dirt road where you'd have to use your best guess based on a compass and maybe get your car exterior scraped by some bushes en route.

This is a metaphor for the brain's potential neural pathways. The thought you've had the MOST is the easiest to think—it's been well paved. No finicky bushes threatening your car's paint job. This is why changing how you think is so challenging at first; it's opting for the back roads consciously, rather than just going down the easy route of the major highway.

So, back to the belief in unluckiness. A continued thought has built out a strong neural pathway in the brain. This makes it far easier to keep thinking "I'm unlucky" than to "switch routes" and think "I'm lucky."

This big, thick neural pathway of unluckiness also helps the brain's reticular activating system look for evidence to CONFIRM this initial belief—that's our confirmation bias again. If someone believes, says, and thinks that they're unlucky repeatedly, they're going to keep attracting unlucky circumstances and noticing unlucky happenings—because it's what their brain is tuned in to look for and attract. In fact, even if they had something objectively "lucky" happen to them, they'd dismiss it, minimize it, or not count it as evidence AGAINST their self-proclaimed unluckiness. The more they experience proof and evidence that they're "unlucky," the thicker the neural pathway becomes. And the easier it is to think they're unlucky. So on, and so forth, round and around, self-fulfilling prophecy.

Remember: the thickness of a neural pathway depends on how often the thought occurs and how many connected experiences have been had.

For every statement and belief on your list, you have a host of accompanying experiences, thoughts, and observations to back up that belief. If I told you to PROVE to me that you always experience scarcity in your finances, you'd have many past scarcity-ridden experiences to back it up. If I told you to PROVE to me that you always fall for the avoidant type in romantic relationships, you could dig up several juicy anecdotes about emotionally unavailable lovers from memory lane who fit the bill. And if I told you to PROVE to me that you have an amazing creative streak and can get into a creative flow quite easily, the same thing would once again be true, and maybe you'd even show me your portfolio of creations.

Because you're used to thinking these thoughts and experiencing these experiences, it's what you're always attracting more of. More evidence for the story you have about yourself. It's the domino effect—the same way an evening of listening to a motivational podcast and making a new vision board leads to more inspiration and excitement, a lifetime of believing and affirming that you'll never get out of debt or you're definitely going to win an Oscar will lead to experiences of the same energy, respectively. Which thought is more empowering to think? How does each story impact you? Do you like how it makes you feel, and the fall of dominoes it's setting into motion when activated? Which stories will you keep, and embolden? And which have GOT to go, so you can live the life you've always dreamed of?

Bringing awareness to our day-to-day life is the most powerful way to identify our patterns. Now that you're aware that today could change everything simply through a shift in your thoughts and attention, you know where to start to shift. If it feels like you're faking it at first, don't worry—this book is heavily rooted in actually rewiring the subconscious mind so you start to truly believe your new affirmations and identity. But in the meantime, I want you to go back to your statement list of experiences and beliefs and do some poking around. Let's start some investigative work, just to prime our minds. We'll be doing lots of investigative work over the course of this book as I teach you the Subconscious Breakthrough Formula, so putting our detective hats on now will start our momentum in that direction.

Unpacking the Story

Let's imagine that someone's statement was "I hate my job." And, true to form, they have such a lengthy list of reasons WHY they hate it so much that they could talk our ears off about it. Every single day, they *expect* to hate their job because they've *been* hating it—no one says, "Just kidding! I bet I'm going to totally LOVE this disaster of a workplace today!"—and the more they hate it, the more they find new reasons to hate it, whether it's a gossipy coworker, extra workload always piled on them, or a strict set of office rules. The actual "hating the job" may be job-specific—*but it's also possible it's a learned behavior.* It's vital that we learn to understand the difference. If it's job-specific, we have a solution on our hands! Let's start job hunting! But if we start to pull it back and realize that really *every* job has been equally horrendous and stressful *to us,* albeit in different ways and featuring different characters, it may be because of a deeper belief and expectation.

Perhaps they've always thought of work as challenging and soul-sucking because their parents always did, and that's what's been modeled for them. Their dad would always be disgruntled coming home from work, muttering something under his breath about how he's working his life away in a thankless job. This person was raised in the belief system that work is *supposed to be unfulfilling,* and so they're always looking for evidence of just that. And the more evidence they accumulate, the more true it becomes. A self-fulfilling prophecy. If they already believe it's supposed to be hard, they'll just continue to find reasons to verify that (thank you, reticular activating system), and it will all become harder, with more evidence of how hard it is . . . and on and on. Whew! Do we see how stories get started?

We want to find the root cause of our stories for each statement. Think of stories as your evidence. If you were proving each of your statements in a court of law, what are the main experiences you would bring up?

I love using examples to jog your brain in the right direction, so here are some ideas of statements and potential stories or points of evidence.

Statement: I never stick to my fitness habits beyond a month tops.

Evidence: Last January I had a New Year's resolution to work out four times a week and I gave up by the time February rolled around because of a few cloudy days and a realllllyyy enticing TV show I started watching. I just stopped wanting to go to the gym when my couch felt so cozy and the weather felt so blah. Come to think of it, I've never really stayed consistent for that long. I always start out motivated then slowly lose the motivation.

Statement: I feel super valued at work.

Evidence: My boss is always so positive in my performance reviews, and I'm great friends with my coworkers who really care about my opinion. We've all been bonding so much at work happy hour over margs and guac. I got a promotion last year and I'm already on track for another!

Statement: I don't trust myself in love because I always go back to my toxic situationship.

Evidence: I swore I was done with him to my friends, then six weeks later he texted me that he missed me and I folded like a bad poker hand. And then I blocked his number after the next "breakup," but unblocked it to wish him a happy birthday, to be the bigger person and all. Which sparked communication all over again. And on and on. I always swear I won't, then do it anyway. I feel like I can't trust myself.

As you go throughout your life, you have all of these statements and accompanying evidence rattling around in your head, affecting your mood and your point of focus . . . positively or negatively. As you begin the miraculous process of changing your entire life, I want you to start to play the role of the observer. What makes you feel better? What makes you feel worse? Track your best days over this coming week. What mood are you in on those days, and what did you do differently to cause that mood? How did that mood change your behavior? What sustained that mood, and what turned it around—for better or for worse?

Part of this is monitoring your thoughts as well. If a breakup song comes on in the elevator that reminds you of your ex, notice that shift in your mood, then tell yourself, "This is an old story I'm releasing." When you show up to the workout class you signed up for to be more consistent in fitness, tell yourself, "I'm doing a great job staying committed to this empowering story."

Start to filter your thoughts and behaviors through the lens of a detective understanding how your story, represented by your statements, is playing out in your life. And know that whatever is disempowering about the story—even if it feels like it's every single part—is about to be easily and naturally released, rewired, and rewritten through the Subconscious Breakthrough Formula.

The Brain and Heart Connection

As I'm sure you've experienced many times in your life, there is a direct connection between the thoughts we think and the emotions we feel. Negative thoughts can spark negative emotions, and positive thoughts can spark positive emotions. And it's also the reverse: the way we FEEL can spark thoughts related to those feelings. We are more likely to think negatively when we're already in a bad mood, which is what can lead us into a total spiral.

The HeartMath Institute has conducted extremely fascinating research on exactly this by studying how the heart responds to emotions. The goal is "heart coherence," which is when the heart is beating in a smooth, regular pattern. This happens when we are experiencing positive emotions. This could range from extreme joy and euphoria on the best day of your life to just a peaceful moment of contentment, snuggled up with your favorite mug of tea as the rain pitter-patters outside.

On the other hand, the heart's pattern can be quite irregular and erratic in the presence of strong negative emotions. Think about the last time you were extremely angry, or if you were going through a season of heartbreak. Your heart actually beats differently because of these emotions, which can be measured in your HRV, heart rate variability.

Why this is so important: when the heart is in a state of coherence, it actually improves our cognitive function. Although it's caused BY positive emotions, it also creates MORE positive emotions. This synchronization of the body and mind also decreases stress levels, and leads to improved focus, concentration, and clarity.

We've all experienced the opposite, when our hearts are "incoherent" because of the strong negative emotions. We're in a frenzy, we can't think straight, and we make decisions on an impulse that we sometimes end up regretting. Like snapping at someone we love and saying something we don't mean. Or pressing send on a heated email to a coworker before we've calmed down.

Part of understanding that today is the day that can change everything is realizing that the power is in your hands! I know emotions can feel big—which is why learning about EFT Tapping, the life-altering technique I mentioned earlier, in part 2 will change SO much for you. But there are also a few steps you can take to achieve heart coherence now and on a regular basis and experience a shift in your thoughts as a result.

1. Do some deep breathing. I know, this sounds so basic, like the beginning of every yoga or meditation class you've ever taken. But it can help immensely, and you'll feel it immensely. Even right now. Nothing fancy is required. Just deepen into your breath.

   When we breathe intentionally and deeply, we signal to our bodies that all is well because it activates the vagus nerve. This stimulates the parasympathetic nervous system, which helps us to deeply relax via a decrease in our heart rate, blood pressure, and stress hormone levels.

   For the sake of heart coherence, you can also imagine that as you breathe deeply, it's creating easy, flowing, warm movement around your heart space. Imagine breathing fresh oxygen into your heart space, cleansing and warm, then imagine that your exhale releases any funky energy. Pro tip: set a timer to go off a few times a day for just one minute of deep breathing.

2. Bring it back to the heart—with some cardio! Getting the heart pumping really helps here, even if it's just going for a fast-paced walk. There's nothing better than that post-workout feeling, because endorphins are "feel good" chemicals. Your heart LOVES to work on your behalf and experience extra joy after a great workout! I also see physical exercise as a form of cleansing out stagnant energy in the body and pressing the restart button, creating heat in the body and dissolving any stuck energy through movement.

3. Deepen into the heart space with gratitude. Once again, this sounds so simple and small but can make a world of difference. Create a practice where every single morning, you write down three things you're grateful for, or do a brief gratitude meditation every day. I really like to just mentally review my day as I'm falling asleep and feel gratitude for all the happy moments and things that went well. It matters! Neuroimaging has shown that gratitude practices have BIG results. Researcher and neuroscientist

Dr. Glenn R. Fox found through these neuroimaging scans that gratitude activates the part of our brain that is associated with the "reward system," which means it helps us feel satisfaction, as if we accomplished something. And we did! Life accomplishes a lot for us, and there's so much to be grateful for.

Research published in the *Journal of Health Psychology* found that individuals who wrote in a gratitude journal before bedtime reported better sleep and increased feelings of well-being, and I can definitely attest to this. Guiding our brain in the direction of gratitude strengthens our reticular activating system to seek out more evidence that there's so much to be grateful for. You'll fall asleep in a deeper state of peace, excited for the next day.

It is very difficult to hold both gratitude and worry at the same time.
Let gratitude win; it's more productive and feels better.

CHAPTER REVIEW AND EXERCISES

TL;DR (jk, please read!)

• Today can be the day that changes your life forever simply through a shift in your PERSPECTIVE. (I'm about to give you some fun ideas on how to start to do this.)

• There is always *sooooo* much more happening around you than meets the eye, or the ears, or the conscious interpretation. And this means . . .

• OPPORTUNITY IS OUT THERE. Not out yonder over the horizon, but literally right here. What you seek is seeking YOU. But you have to *actually* seek it through your conscious attention and focus. You have to order the package for it to arrive on your front doorstep.

• What you get in your reality unfolds from the story you're telling yourself, which may be unconscious. We bring it into the conscious mind by unpacking the story.

• Seek to understand the basis and origin of the stories that are at play in each area of your life. Over this book, we'll release and rewire the core evidence for the stories you could live without, and we'll embolden the stories that are serving you.

• Begin to regulate your emotions with your breathing, some cardio, and some gratitude practices as mini-additions to your day that can start to change the energy waves of your life.

Perspective Shift Ideas

I love to have fun with all of this, especially for big new concepts. Here are some ideas of new perspectives you could try adopting, for as little as thirty minutes to as long as a week (or the rest of your life if you really like it).

• Imagine everyone who shows up in your reality today was sent by the Universe to BLESS YOU. Even the stranger next to you on the train who doesn't say a word. Don't question it—they're bringing magical fairy dust into your life with or without a life-changing conversation.

• Imagine the words you hear in passersby's conversations or come across in a quote today is a *sign* sent to help you on your way and tell you exactly what you need to hear and know for this new journey. You'll know which are FOR YOU when you hear them or read them.

• Choose a day when you'll infuse fun everywhere you go, in everything you do. Douse it in FUN, whatever that looks like for you. This doesn't mean blow off your responsibilities and hit an amusement park (unless you just got a surge of OMG, I NEED TO DO THAT IMMEDIATELY! from reading that). Rather, take it as a fun assignment to see how many small choices you can add into your day that are ridiculously fun. Like wearing a big fuzzy hat or dressing up extra fancy. Or "accidentally" blasting "Hollaback Girl" at work to switch up the vibe for everyone. Or asking your neighbor or a coworker or an old friend if they want to grab a quick ice cream cone with you later.

• Today is the day of Magical Coffee—or Magical Water, or Magical Diet Coke. Whatever beverage you sip the MOST throughout the day (can you tell mine is coffee from the sheer number of coffee mentions just in chapter 1?) has been magically infused with extra good luck and extra creativity. The best ideas you've ever had are entering your bloodstream with every sip. And you're getting luckier and luckier and luckier as you hydrate.

• Exercise leads to old story goodbyes (a poem). I like to imagine when I'm walking, running, biking, or moving in any way, shape, or form that the exercise is working the old story out of my DNA. If you've just decided to release the story you've been living by about your alleged unluckiness in love, for example, imagine in your upcoming exercise that every drop of sweat is releasing it. Imagine those endorphins are really your cells throwing a party: "Woooohoooo! That old sad story is gone at last! Ding dong the (sitch) is dead!"

• Finally, review your list of statements, and rewrite the ones you'd like to experience differently. For example, if one is "I'm seldom consistent with my habits," write what you would rather believe. Maybe this is "I am becoming more consistent with the habits that serve me." These statements may feel as far as possible from the truth right now, but you'll learn later in this book how to write affirmations and utilize them for subconscious rewiring. This is a powerful first step in that direction and for starting to craft a new story with your magic wand!

CHAPTER 2

I ENVISION, THEN I SEE

When I first moved to New York City, I became infatuated with the idea of a penthouse apartment. I mean, hello, luxury, am I right? Every single morning, I'd close my eyes and visualize my dream life while listening to the song "Time" by Hans Zimmer. Images would flash through my mind's eye related to my dreams and vision board items, and one image began to form over time: a sweeping penthouse apartment. I'd walk in the front door to a sprawling, rectangular space that was half living room, half kitchen, with big windows and a glorious view of the Empire State Building. I imagined luxurious furniture, a dark purple couch. A vibrant yet deeply royal space. It felt so expansive and fun to visualize this as a "one day" manifestation, since at the time I was living in a little studio apartment and couldn't see myself in a place like that for *at least* several years unless I were to spontaneously win the lottery.

But still, the visualization subsisted. To me, it wasn't so much about actually manifesting it (again, it felt so far away) as it was about playful make believe and imagination, like when I was a kid, daydreaming for hours in my room. The more I visualized it, the more I could feel the *energy* of a penthouse apartment. It made everything sparkle a bit more, like it was broadening my horizons to imagine living in such a beautiful space. It started to become so real from my frequent visualizations that I talked about it to a couple of my best friends at lunch in Manhattan one day.

"I feel like it's coming, even though that makes no sense whatsoever!" I laughed, and my very supportive friends nodded in affirmation. They know that visualization is no joke.

Later in the lunch, the waiter brought a full cake to our table, saying it had been sent "for Haley's birthday." My birthday wasn't until the next month, and he didn't say who sent it, which was extremely odd. We all laughed over the mystery cake, thanked the Universe for it, and enjoyed it, luxuriating in a happy, albeit confusing experience. Still, to this day, no one has stepped forward and said they sent the cake. We decided that maybe it was a mistake, like a birthday cake meant for a different table also under a "Haley" reservation, even though the waiter had insisted it was for us. But does the Universe really make mistakes? *Aggressive wink.*

The next month, I had a marketing partnership with the Langham Hotel in New York City, timed to my birthday. I'd seen from their Instagram that whenever it was a guest's birthday, they'd send a tray of pink macarons to the room, and for some reason this really spoke to me! I was so excited, envisioning my little tray of pink macarons.

On the eve of my birthday I arrived at the hotel, beaming with excitement and gratitude for the entire experience. When I checked in, the receptionist smiled at me and said, "We saved a *very* nice room for you." I internally squealed, imagining my tray of pink macarons. She handed the room key over to me, and I headed up to the room number listed.

When I arrived at the top floor and followed the numbered signs to my room, I was guided down a designated corridor with double doors. I looked up at the room number, and printed plainly against the wall were just the words *Presidential Suite*.

"Oh, this can't be it," I thought to myself, and I turned around to find the right room. But the sign on the wall with my room number was still pointing toward that ONE set of double doors. I blinked a few times, returned to the Presidential Suite sign, and saw the number right there: it *was* my room. I *gasped*.

I took a deep breath as I scanned my room key to open the door, already in a state of disbelief that I was about to *be* in—let alone *stay* in—a hotel's presidential suite for the first time! And when I opened the door...

It was my *Exact. Penthouse. Visualization.* I have chills even reflecting on it as I write this. Believe me when I tell you it's been one of the only moments of my life to date when I've almost fallen to the ground from absolute shock. Every single square inch of this suite was exactly what I had conjured in my morning ritual visualization. The sprawling rectangular room. Half living room, half dining room. Dark purple furniture. Floor-to-ceiling windows. I couldn't process it. It felt like a mental glitch between the real and imagined. I'd imagined and mentally rehearsed it so many times "just for fun"—and now, somehow, I was in the space?! It had quite literally materialized out of my own mental picture.

I had never seen images of the Langham until the marketing opportunity arose—which was weeks after the lunch where I'd told my friends my visualization felt so real and so close. I didn't even know that the Langham had a presidential suite, and I'd never seen a picture of it, either. This was *entirely of my own creation*. And, to make it even more magical, I remembered I got a little *wink wink* from the Universe at lunch the previous month when the waiter had sent out a mystery birthday cake just shortly after I'd told my friends that I felt like the penthouse was coming.

In retrospect, I don't believe that I was the sole architect of this penthouse experience as I was visualizing it. In other words, as magical as I think we all are, it would be a little bit of a reach to assume that in just about two months, a whole penthouse wing of my exact design and specifications could get whipped up on the top floor of a hotel in New York City. But I do believe I was "receiving" the image. It was a possibility, a potential—a real penthouse that I would ultimately have access to for two beloved nights. The more I ruminated on the details and the way it made me feel, the closer I pulled it to my experience. I didn't know that's what I was doing at the time, but it revealed itself perfectly.

So now, I like to think of visualization as allowing your mind to travel to different potential realities laid out in front of you. You may not have seen certain spaces before, or you might not be aware of certain people or opportunities, but that's the fun of visualization. Surprises arise as you allow yourself to daydream like when you were a kid. You may discover new insights about what you want—or you'll just have a fun, eyes-closed experience envisioning what you've always known you wanted.

Another example of this is a ten-minute meditation I did just a couple years ago when I was testing out the idea of a "quantum leap," which is the concept that we can "leap" to another reality or quantum field by imagining ourselves there and feeling the emotions associated. If I told you to close your eyes and really FEEL the magic of a desired future where you had your dream career, for example, the theory is that this is itself a quantum leap because you're FEELING and SEEING what you want as if it's actually happening.

Anyway, when I began experimenting with this, I had recently begun putting out music as a singer and songwriter, and I had just been thinking how cool it would be to one day have my own cover of a Spotify playlist. I'd see recommended playlists like "Today's Top Hits" with pictures of Taylor Swift or Drake on the front, and I'd fantasize about one day being able to be *that* influential with my music that my own face would be on the cover.

So I allowed myself to imagine it for just those ten minutes. I imagined the fulfillment of knowing my music was reaching its audience and making people feel things or enjoy themselves, helping them heal. I focused on how fun it is to make music and my intention to keep reaching more ears. I really, REALLY felt it.

The very next day, I got an Instagram DM from a friend—a screenshot of something that had shown up on her Spotify that day. Her Release

Radar, the weekly playlist of new music that Spotify's algorithm personalizes for each listener . . . with MY picture as the cover of the playlist! I had never seen this before, and my jaw hit the floor. I began to feel that familiar tingle, the *How is this really happening . . . ?* moment from my penthouse experience a few years prior. Throughout the day, I received more and more messages and screenshots of the same from other friends and followers. This wasn't a fluke! People who had previously listened to my music were seeing *me* on the cover of a playlist on the Spotify homepage. Other artists as big as Taylor Swift (my girl!) were also on the playlist for some of those users, yet somehow the algorithm had put MY picture on the cover. UNREAL.

Clearly I was onto something with this "quantum leap" form of a visualization—which again, means you're feeling the strong, positive emotions associated with what you see in your mind's eye. I decided to give myself a little challenge to see just how far I could take this magic, and decided I'd do TWO quantum leap visualizations a day for a week straight. The goal: to change my energetic state so much that I'd invite in a lot of magic . . . and it absolutely worked. That week was one of the most exhilarating weeks of my life on an emotional level—everything felt tenfold more exciting. I remember arriving at my recording studio that week and telling my producer that I felt like I had something really big and exciting to tell him, but I couldn't put my finger on what it was. Then I realized my brain just thought I did because it had been doing such a great job visualizing huge music wins and performances!

As part of this experiment, I set the intention at the beginning of the challenge that I'd be shown blue sparkle lights somewhere in my reality if I was actually making a difference and changing my life with these profound visualizations. I'd chosen blue sparkle lights because of the moving graphic on one of my favorite online videos to focus on while visualizing, which looked like blue sparkle lights, surrounded by little shapes in different colors. If THAT could show up in my actual living reality, that would be quite the sign. In my mind, I thought maybe I'd stumble across a string of blue lights out and about in the city, trying to make sense of how that could come together and be my sign off the screen.

As the week wrapped up, I still hadn't seen anything resembling blue string lights, but I kept the faith. I spontaneously went to see a movie that weekend, and at the very end of the movie, the screen lit up with blue string lights. But not just blue string lights. A bunch of little shapes in different colors danced around the blue lights in the film, very closely resembling the moving graphic of my visualization video. I couldn't believe my eyes. It had been such a last-minute decision to even go to that movie, and it never crossed my mind that the sign I was looking for would show up in a film.

By now, you're probably grasping that I've had some pretty wild experiences with what I've seen in my head transpiring into my reality in glamorous and fun ways. These are just a few of my favorite stories because they represent wishes near and dear to my heart and a life that really reflects the vision board I've had for a decade. I share these stories to help you feel the magic, too, and to jog your memory on times that perhaps you visualized something before it happened or came to pass. Whether you visualize religiously or you're new to all of this, this chapter will give you an invaluable tool for crafting the life of your dreams, all in your mind.

It Is Magic, but It Isn't Just Magic

The research on the power of visualization always gives me chills. This has been studied in depth in many different ways. One that's always boggled my mind is a study done where two groups of volunteers were told to *just visualize* mental contractions: one of their little finger, the other of their elbows. This was to be done five days a week, fifteen minutes a day. A third group was told to actually go ahead and train to increase finger abduction. To be clear: the first two groups were visualizing this, no actual weights lifted. Then, a group of six did actual physical training with finger abductions for the same training cadence.

The results were staggering: the group that *just visualized* finger contractions experienced an increase in their finger abduction strength by 35 percent, without any physical work actually done. 35 percent! The group that mentally trained their elbow flexion strength experienced a strength increase of 13.5 percent. All from the comfort of their couch! Sign me up for THAT mental workout class. Of course, the group that actually did the physical training experienced a 53 percent increase in finger abduction strength, but still.

Many accomplished athletes credit visualization as a key component of their success. Bob Bowman, coach of Olympic gold medalist Michael Phelps, shared that one of the most important parts of race prep has always been visualization, saying that the race is visualized *hundreds* of times in Phelps's head before he ever gets into the pool. The reason for this is to get his body into a state of autopilot from so much mental rehearsal, so when it's "go time" with the thrill of the race and the loud buzzers and the pressure of onlookers and camera crews, his body does what it knows it's supposed to do. Just like breathing.

Dr. Joe Dispenza is a prominent figure in the fields of neuroscience, meditation, and personal transformation. He is known for his work in exploring the connection between mind, body, and consciousness and harnessing the power of the mind to create positive change in one's life. Dr. Dispenza's work emphasizes the role of thoughts, emotions, and beliefs in shaping our reality.

Dispenza states frequently that the brain can't actually tell the difference between a *real* experience and an *imagined* one (of course this is dependent on how vividly we imagine it). Mentally rehearsing something like a race ahead of time actually works as a form of *practice*. This doesn't mean Phelps didn't do all the other necessary training and prep; these visualizations were ancillary. He still showed up to practice and gave his all. But he made sure to mentally rehearse every race as many times as possible in exactly the way he wanted it to happen, and because his brain experienced all those mental rehearsals as *real* experiences, he was deeply prepared for success. And it paid off, again and again!

Gold medalist skier Lindsey Vonn says the exact same thing. She has said that she would visualize the same race over one hundred times before she ever got to the gate, mentally going through every single turn in her head. Again and again. Record-breaking Olympic gold medalist gymnast Simone Biles has shared that visualization is a "crucial part" of her training. And legendary tennis player Serena Williams has said, "Visualize success with such clarity it becomes inevitable."

Visualization aids performance—but it also aids manifestation in all its forms, bringing to reality what you want to experience. Famously, the actor Jim Carrey wrote himself a check for $10 million for "acting services rendered" back before he ever booked a gig. He was only twenty-three years old, and far from successful. In fact, he was broke. He dated the check for ten years in the future, then he carried this check with him in his wallet every single day for those ten years. It helped him keep the faith through many disappointments and ups and downs. And almost exactly ten years later, he landed his role in *Dumb and Dumber* . . . for $10 million. He has shared that he still carries that check in his wallet as a reminder of his power as a creator, even though it's now creased and worn.

APPLYING VISUALIZATION TO YOUR LIFE

On a micro level, you can begin experiencing the awesome power of visualization in small ways simply by imagining how you want something to go. If you have a big meeting or interview coming up, visualize the best-case scenario for every minute of the meeting. The handshake. The smiles. Feeling confident. Just clicking with the other person. The feeling afterward, when you text your friend and say, "It went so well!" Play it out as many times as you can as a form of preparation.

The same works in high-stakes moments, like an exam or a performance. Keep making mind movies or mental rehearsals of how you want it to go. Imagine how you'll feel at every step—confidence as you effortlessly hit the high note in a singing performance, or thinking "Wow, I'm acing this!" as you charge through an exam. Your body feeling strong and fast as you whiz past the halfway point of the marathon ahead of your average pace.

It's important for me to re-emphasize here that visualization should never replace the other actions required to knock something out of the park. You should still study, practice, train, and do everything you need to do to be your personal best. But the visualization component will help you show up feeling extra confident, and your body will have a higher chance of shifting into the rehearsed autopilot of success if it's been mentally rehearsed enough times.

Some other fun ways to apply visualization:

In the morning before you get out of bed, prime your brain for the best possible day by making a mind movie of the day you want to have. Mentally survey everything on your calendar and to-do list, then imagine the best possible way each event could go. You can also do this by fast-forwarding to the end of the day and imagining yourself lying in bed that night. What do you want to think as you look back at the day? How do you want to feel?

An example: "Tonight I want to feel like the day was so productive, fun, and energized. I'll be sleepy from a day where I gave my all, but there will be a spark of magic and excitement for tomorrow!" Or: "Tonight I want to feel rejuvenated after a great day off. I want my nervous system to feel completely at peace."

If you ever have a travel day ahead of you, try the same visualization tricks. Air travel in particular always comes with so many contingencies and uncertainties. Visualize yourself gliding through every step of your journey and having the best time. I've done this numerous times and I'm always amazed at the difference in my travel day.

On a recent travel day, I was worried about how long the bag-check line would be, and then how long the security line would be, since I was flying on a busy day. I mentally pictured the smoothest possible travel experience, with minimal waiting. When I arrived at the airport, there were only a couple people ahead of me in the baggage-check line. As I took my place, something wild happened: a massive line began to form BEHIND me. Easily twenty-five other people started filing in. "Lucky timing," I thought to myself, because I've primed myself to believe I am *lucky!*

Then, I got to the security line and just a few people were ahead of me. As I was standing there waiting, I was completely unaware of it—but the same thing began to happen. As I turned the corner to present my ID to the TSA agent, I did a double take at the line that had once again formed behind me—a SEA of new travelers had appeared. Was I on the fast track, or what?! Now I always do this ahead of time for anything! Oprah has said, "Create the highest, grandest vision possible for your life, because you become what you believe." Whether it's rehearsing an upcoming performance, match, meet, date, or interview, or simply rehearsing the best-case scenario for your life, the power is in your hands.

WHY THIS HAPPENS

Remember my earlier statement that visualization helps us to select a potential reality? At any given moment, multiple paths are stretched out in front of us, like a tree with many branches. What unfolds next is highly dependent on our personal choices, including:

• Our actions
• Our point of focus
• Our feelings
• Our expectations

Visualization is one of the most powerful tools to prime us toward what we *most want* to happen next, because it shifts all of the above. Let's get into it.

Our Actions

We take actions because of what feels like the best thing for us to do in a given moment and what we believe the action will do for us. For example, imagine you want to work out tomorrow morning, but that means you'll have to wake up at 5:00 a.m. to squeeze in a run or some weightlifting before work. Whether or not you actually take that action depends on a number of factors. When the alarm goes off and it's still dark out, it may feel best to just roll over and go back to sleep at that moment. But if you've already primed yourself via visualization to think through all the goodness that's on the other side of a morning workout, you'll be more inclined to get out of bed.

In order for you to actually roll out of bed and stumble in the dark to put on your workout clothes even though your eyes are heavy and your bed always feels extra snuggly and warm when you have to get out of it too soon, you would have to be genuinely motivated in every cell of your being to resist the comfortable and forge ahead. This motivation comes from mental rehearsal. Maybe you imagined getting a big kick of endorphins and momentum in the second half of your workout, then finishing right as the sun rose. Then feeling so energized and accomplished all day, with that sensational post-workout feeling. Or maybe you'd be looking forward to your post-workout green juice or ten-minute sauna break. Or all of the above!

If you had not primed yourself to feel excited for this via the visualization, it's highly likely that your desire for sleep would have overridden your motivation.

This goes beyond daily choices and habits. I am a singer and songwriter, and I always find that after I've done a very exciting visualization of performing my songs onstage, I feel a huge boost to work on a new song that day. If you're frequently visualizing the things you want most for your life, you'll feel more motivated to do what it takes to get there. It will get you into the energy of already HAVING the life you dream of. Remember, for your future self, these actions are second nature—that version of you has already aced them!

If you're imagining an explosion of abundance like your sales dashboard doubling overnight from a potent ad initiative, you're more likely to film another video that day highlighting the benefits of your product.

If you're imagining walking down the aisle in the South of France to marry your soulmate to the tune of your favorite love song (a *Bridgerton*-worthy string-quartet rendition for extra tear-jerker effect, of course), you're more likely to put yourself out there and hit that singles event or give a few people on your dating app a chance.

If you're imagining your first big book signing and dozens of readers telling you how much they LOVED your book, you're more likely to sit down and pour some words onto the page!

Our Point of Focus

One of the most powerful and true statements is "What you focus on expands," which is why I'm writing it down YET again in this book. This is the reticular activating system at work, which you know all about by now. And it's true for anything.

Have you ever gotten caught up in a personal drama? Who am I kidding—we all have, obvs. Maybe it was a tiff with a friend or a coworker, or that one dude coming back around yet again. A situation like this is incredibly irritating—and we *keep focusing on it* as a result. We tell all our friends about it. We deliberate on it. We have mental arguments to workshop our comebacks. We look up related articles or podcast episodes. This is all in a subconscious attempt to rectify the situation because these actions make us feel in control. But when you inevitably look back, you'll see that those days or that entire week was indelibly marked by that situation, because it was SO in your point of focus that it influenced everything else.

Visualization is a way to shift gears or change the channel in our mind. It's an opportunity to reset our point of focus. And believe me, I've definitely had my moments when I've sat down to visualize and my mind kept hijacking the moment to overthink something else I'd been thinking about prior. Sometimes, guiding the mind to visualize what we want is a lot like trying to tug an overexcited puppy away from the tastiest-smelling cactus it's ever encountered on its walk.

Even just a quick visualization of the type of day (or *life*) you'd like to have can shift your focus enough that you experience something different. Think of your focus as the water and sunshine that make a seed grow. You always have a few different proverbial pots on your windowsill. There's one for some good ol' fashioned drama, which is basically just a black hole of your time and energy unless there's something you can do about it to alleviate it (in which case, DO IT!). Then, there's another pot, filled with fertile soil blessed by the Universe, for your Big Life Dream. Which seeds will grow? The ones you water with your focus.

Here's a hack: when you notice your focus meandering off the path of what you WANT to call in, say "SHIFT!" (either mentally or out loud) and immediately come back to the present moment by putting your focus on three items around you. One, two, three—let your eyes focus on the details of each, whether it's a cloud in the sky or a pen on the table or your own polished fingernail. You can also take a few deep breaths to regulate. This is what's called a "pattern interrupt," which we'll get into in great depth when we're ready to apply subconscious breakthroughs to your entire life a little later in the book.

This shift is so critical because focus gains momentum. It's easier to KEEP focusing on something once you're already focused on it. Imagine that you're having a heated vent session with a friend at dinner, telling them with only increasing fervor how RIDICULOUS this one situation is, gesturing dramatically (and dangerously) with your fork in hand as you finish your salad. Then, your entrée comes, but you're too focused on your story and your venting to even taste your food.

"Wow, that was delicious!" your friend says as the meal wraps up, and you realize you hadn't slowed your roll on your Great Vent long enough to even decide if YOUR meal was delicious as you were eating it!

Focus amplifies whatever it's aimed at, making it bigger and bigger and bigger. It then blocks out anything in your periphery, making it even easier to stay focused despite distractions begging for your attention. So if shifting your focus feels incredibly difficult at first, don't worry. It will become easier to pivot to the new point of focus as long as you keep trying and build that momentum.

The other exciting thing about focus is that we get more of what we focus on. This is obviously NOT exciting if we're focusing on what we DON'T want to experience. Have you ever noticed that when you're running late, everything seems like it's going so much slower? Traffic feels like it's moving at a snail's pace. Every light turns red just as you approach it and every car you get stuck behind seems to be driven by the world's most relaxed driver, who clearly must think the speed limit is half of what it really is. This isn't because the whole world is out to get you and MAKE you late—it's because you're focused on the concept of being short on time, so you keep getting more of that! If you hadn't been in any rush, you wouldn't have noticed any of these extra delays. You'd be happily sipping your beverage, blasting your tunes, thinking about your plans that night, and you'd arrive at your destination without any thought about how long it took.

And if you're focused on opportunity, you'll get more of THAT, just like my story about stumbling into my first paid speaking engagement. I'm an entrepreneur and a creative, and I have a lot of pots on the stove at any given moment—my business, my coaching clients, my music—and I've noticed the most fascinating pattern: wherever I'm MOST focused, flowers bloom. I'll go through streaks where I'm ultra focused on my music, for example, and that's always when I get random music opportunities or have song ideas come to me all day long. It's very difficult for me to brainstorm new ideas for my business if I'm focused solely on my music for a week because it's just not my point of focus. And vice versa; I'll experience some serious writer's block with songwriting when I'm most focused on my business. Wherever I turn my focus is where I nurture the seed. It's the water and the sunshine.

Our Feelings

Our point of focus can affect our feelings, and the two have a very interdependent relationship. Because sometimes our feelings *hijack* our focus. Once, I spent a weeklong vacation in Miami, which is one of my favorite places in the entire world. I always call it my happy place because I feel my best when I'm there. It was an absolutely beautiful week and all I had planned for each day was a leisurely breakfast, pool time, a beachside bike ride, swimming in the waves, a workout, and a fun dinner out. My personal heaven!

During this particular week, there was a snafu with one of my physical product launches. I had partnered with someone I'd worked with prior, but somehow, there were several miscommunications and customers weren't getting their products, which had been his responsibility. I value my customers and their experience above all else, and this entire situation was causing a deep panic in me. There was nothing I could do except ask for what I needed and open up communication channels with my customers to let them know I would do everything in my power to make it right. And then I had to wait for the other parties involved to step up.

My feelings about the situation clouded the whole week. Even in the moments when I had done everything I could, I couldn't stop thinking about it and fixating. I remember going on a bike ride, unable to even get a full deep breath or take in the perfect ocean breeze and sparkling blue water in my line of sight. My mind was racing thinking of contingency plans, replaying what had occurred, and ruminating on how this could even happen.

Even though there was nothing else to be done at that stage, my anxiety and worry infiltrated every single moment of the trip because my focus was on the situation. And that focus only created MORE anxiety and worry. Everything felt like it was going wrong. I look back now, of course, and think I handled the action items available to me like a boss— but ALL the extra panic? Incredibly unnecessary, and it basically ruined the entire trip. This is a situation where visualizing what I would've rather had happen instead would have helped.

On the flip side, a similar situation happened a few months earlier, but with my music. One of my songs was taken down from streaming services because I trusted the wrong marketing team to help me promote it, and they had been utilizing some dishonest promotional techniques. When I realized what had happened and that I'd essentially been scammed, there were a lot of emotions associated. I cried for hours in a frenzy. And to make matters worse, I couldn't figure out how to re-upload the song. The distribution service did not seem to be working, and no one was getting back to me to help. I was spiraling.

But I'll never forget what happened next. My EFT practitioner, dear friend, and mentor, Tiffany (more on her later!), called me to coach me through, and she had me visualize the best-case scenario that could unfold from that moment forward. At first, everything felt made up.

"I guess I could get a hold of someone at the distributor who can help get the song back up?" I said through tears.

"Great!" she said. "Visualize that, but make it *even* better and easier."

So I did. I imagined hearing back from someone very nurturing and attentive who could help the next day, and the entire situation resolving swiftly. I imagined my song back up on streaming services like it never went down, and I imagined my energy field and my music cleansed of anyone dishonest.

To be clear, as I did it, this entire visualization felt too good to be true. I felt like I was absolutely making it up. But as I mentally rehearsed it several times, I actually felt my body calm down and start to embody the way it would feel if it *were* true. Of course, I tapped as well (more on this shortly!), so I started to calm down immensely. I fell asleep feeling peaceful, despite all the uncertainty.

Would it shock you if I told you that the NEXT DAY, my visualization unfolded exactly as I pictured it? A very kind customer service representative from the distribution service got back to my messages, the song went back up like it never left, and no one dishonest has come anywhere close to my music in the years since. All was taken care of. Just like I visualized. I was frankly in awe that the visualization could work considering it felt so impossible the mere night before.

Now I always use visualization to help guide my feelings, especially when I'm worried about something. I'll simply make a mind movie of what I want to have happen. I will also write down the best-case scenario when I'm journaling just because I think that cements it more. And it's fun to read it back later and realize things have turned out pretty darn similar to the best-case scenario I'd written!

Just ask yourself: "What is the BEST way this could unfold from here?" and see how that plays out in your mind. The more you replay it, the more you make it real. And the more you'll calm down and feel all the hope associated.

Our Expectations

What logically follows from our feelings is our expectations. In the example of my Great Song Takedown Crisis, it took a shift in my feelings and my mental rehearsal of the best-case scenario to also shift my *expectations* of what would happen next. Once I'd seen the best-case scenario play out in my head a few times, it *naturally* changed my expectation. This happened on a subconscious level. I didn't have to guide my conscious brain to expect the best-case scenario to unfold; it just felt more likely that that would happen because I'd visualized it so many times. As I fell asleep that night, I soothed any other temporary moments of anxiety with the visualization, contributing to the new feelings of peace in my body.

Remember, Dr. Joe Dispenza says that the brain can't tell the difference between a real and an imagined event. So, it's important to understand how your brain remembers the key details of a real event that has happened. Think about a day you had last week—any day, it doesn't matter. Close your eyes and remember it to the best of your ability. If you were to tell someone else all about the day and try to transport them into the memory, what would you say? Situate yourself in one moment from that day that stands out. Recall any feelings, sights, sounds, and smells about the day. Notice what stands out to you most from replaying this memory; what your brain focuses on most when recalling a moment from your past. It's different for everyone. For example, for me, I am visually dominant and I feel emotions deeply. When I remember something vividly, I'm taken back to what I saw and what I felt.

Then, take another minute right now and make up a *mind movie* of a day in the future when you'll feel content and in awe of all the good that has transpired in your life. It could be any time in the future. Let it be fun. Play up the details. We want to make this visualization similar in intensity and certainty to the *real* memory you just replayed, so imagine it in the way your brain remembers memories. Once again, for me, this means I'm imagining the visuals of this future memory and conjuring what emotions I think I'd feel. You may not have all the details at first, but that's okay; let yourself be in that sweet space of make believe and imagination. What would you see on this day? Hear? Smell? Taste? Feel emotionally, as a result?

Zoom out. Your future memory isn't just about a moment; it's about a life. If you're imagining waking up in your dream home and having a happy Sunday in with your partner and children, play that out. What would you make for breakfast? What type of couch would you sit on for family movie day? How would your coffee taste, and from what coffee machine, in what cup? "Advance remember" it the same way you'd remember something that ALREADY happened. Once it forms in your mind in a way that feels exciting and warm to you, replay the tape. Then again. And again.

Ideally, you can collect multiple "future memories" as scenes you pull on whenever you sit down to visualize. Allow your mind to shift between multiple future scenarios you'd like to live out, soaking in the fullness of each one as you do.

It's my belief that when this is done enough, a visualization becomes second nature, almost an impulse. For years, I would always imagine driving my dream car, and I practiced this mind movie many times, diligently. I could feel my hands on the steering wheel, I could picture the interior of the car, my foot on the gas, that delicious new car smell, and the feeling of exhilaration that I'd DONE IT. Flash forward to the day when I lived out this exact visualization! Only caveat: it was even better than I'd pictured. I hadn't thought to put a gorgeous sunset over the West Side Highway as I drove home in my dream car, or the fact that I'd just returned from a birthday trip in Lake Como and everything felt ultra magical. Nope; the Universe added in those fun details and context for me.

After that day, as I moved forward and continued visualizing, I found that my brain would naturally bring forth the Dream Car Visualization on its own! It was unconscious; it had been so imprinted in my brain that even when I didn't need to visualize it anymore, it would still come to my mind's eye when I relaxed and moved into a visualization space. This is ideal! Of course, I then realized that maybe the reason it kept coming forth (in addition to being so well-practiced) was because now, the "future memory" was a "past memory" and "present memory." I wasn't visualizing driving my dream car at some time in the future anymore; I was just remembering what it's like to drive my car that's parked right downstairs.

Remember that the more you can key into specific details, the more real it becomes to your brain, and suddenly, your brain thinks that this future memory has actually happened. This changes your expectation; it's not a "maybe" anymore, it's as *definite* as a past memory. So of course it would happen in the future!

Neuroplasticity

The reason this happens is because of neuroplasticity, which is the principle that our brain can rewire itself. You are not stuck the way that you are. You are the magic—and you can commence this magic at any time by understanding how your brain works!

The neural pathways in your brain aren't permanent; your brain is ALWAYS changing, whether you're consciously rewiring with visualizations and future mental mind movies or not. Your brain is making new synapse connections with everything you learn. Your perception of love as you navigate relationships and read romance novels. Your increased ease with new skills as you learn how to make edits to your website or practice a new instrument.

One of the best examples of the neuroplasticity of the brain is learning a language. For a while when I was in college, I took Italian on Mondays through Thursdays, and I learned the language quickly. When I went to Italy for a monthlong immersion business program that summer, I was able to practice my Italian with Italians, and at that point, I was so in the flow of my Italian language learning that I was even starting to dream in Italian. I entered a space of such ease with it that it removed the step of mental translation from English to Italian before I spoke or wrote.

However, I stopped taking Italian the following year when I became too busy with my honors thesis. I thought for sure I'd be able to keep it up—by that point, I had beloved Italian songs in my rotation and Italian friends; I was sure I'd learned it so well. But, as you're probably catching on to here . . . I started to lose it! Now, all these years later, I know very little Italian, and even stutter when I try to go beyond "Ciao!" It's almost as if I was never in that flow to begin with. My brain completely lost the neural pathways of the Italian language because I wasn't using them and I hadn't used them for long enough to make them really take hold.

Maybe you have a similar story with a language, an instrument, or a skill set. Unless you're continuously using it and honing it, it's going to fade. You can get it back, but you have to apply focus. Your brain is energy efficient, which means it doesn't want to keep anything that is no longer relevant. Think about when you finished a course in high school or college and still had a stack of miscellaneous papers with all your notes from studying. You probably recycled them when cleaning out your locker or backpack, because you no longer had any use for them.

You already took the final exam. Your brain is doing the same thing all the time, based on the information you're giving it and where you choose to place your attention. This gives more life and momentum to the mind movies of your future when you mentally rehearse them on a continuous basis. But if you don't visualize for several weeks, you'll find it's difficult to get into the same level of detail and emotional attachment as you once achieved.

Know this: Every time you're rehearsing the future mentally, your brain is using the same process it does when it's recalling a memory. It's encoding the related neural pathways with the information. The goal is to make your visualization so real via practice that the neural connection becomes as strong as possible. This will influence your beliefs, expectations, and energy. You'll find that life sparkles with extra promise and possibility when you're visualizing your dream reality more often. The infusion of that magic influences your current reality, even if there's a major gap between where you are and where you want to be.

To tie it all together, let's take you, where you are, right now. You obviously picked up this book to change your life, right? You have things you REALLY want for yourself. You have big dreams. You have an exciting vision board.

If you added visualization into the equation, you could start seeing some major magic unfold within a matter of days. All I'm "assigning" you is a few minutes of visualizations every single day as a bare minimum. Remember, all it took to manifest my penthouse experience was a daily listen to the song "Time" by Hans Zimmer. That song is a mere four minutes and thirty-five seconds long.

Use those few minutes to watch a first-person trailer of the movie of your dream life, pulling up the future scenes you're rehearsing, and allowing each day of visualization to help you deepen into the feelings associated with, and clarify the details of, the future experience. And notice what changes in your life as a result. Notice the shift in your body over the course of the visualization and the new emotions and sensations that arise. Notice how you feel before versus after the visualization. And notice how you feel on the days you *do* take the time to visualize versus the days you forget.

This practice will change your actions because you'll be inspired to start taking more steps forward toward what you want. That could be as small as actually sitting down to brainstorm your business idea for fifteen minutes or as big as purchasing a podcast microphone or starting an application for an MFA program. I promise you, you'll feel more motivated when you've seen it happen in your mind.

It will change your point of focus because it will feel so exciting to envision your dream life. You won't want to stop thinking about it the rest of the day. And if you get distracted and other points of focus arise, you'll just return back to the juicy Trailer of My Dream Magical Life of Excitement and Everything I've Ever Wanted tomorrow when you sit down to visualize again.

What you focus on expands.

This will change your feelings because, once again, it's EXCITING! These visualizations will spark feelings of euphoria. And even in small doses, euphoria can change the course of your life. Everything will sparkle a bit more with hope and possibility. And the more you tend to that, the more it will grow. Because your point of focus only expands, you'll also notice you attract more happy serendipities related to what you visualize. Maybe you'll stumble across a podcast episode related to your goal that shares some great resources or steps you can take, or maybe you'll happen to meet someone who has achieved exactly what you're wanting to do. An opportunity will fall in your lap. This will happen naturally!

You just have to take my word for it—and invest five fun minutes of your life (daily).

And finally, visualization changes your expectations simply by changing your perspective. If you've deep down believed that your dream life borders on impossible, it's likely you've never really allowed yourself to visualize what living it would actually be like! But if you can close your eyes and go through the motions of a life where all your wildest dreams have come true, it will begin to feel more possible simply because it has to. Because I will repeat YET AGAIN: your brain can't tell the difference between a real and an imagined experience. The more it can envision something—even if it feels outlandish—the more possible it will naturally feel, because your brain believes it actually happened just yesterday.

Don't underestimate how quickly things can happen for you because of visualization, too. Selecting a potential ahead of you can shift your reality very quickly—especially paired in tandem with EFT Tapping and subconscious breakthroughs, as we're about to get into. But first, we must take everything a step deeper: into the depths of the subconscious mind.

CHAPTER REVIEW AND EXERCISES
TL;DR

- Visualization is daydreaming a whole new reality. HAVE FUN WITH IT! Let it be like "make believe" when you were a kid.

- The more you can *feel* the visualization and play up your emotions, the better! This skyrockets your vibration and makes your brain more convinced that the visualization is *actually* happening, which makes it more likely to manifest, thanks to our mirror neurons.

- Many successful individuals tout the power of visualization for achieving goals, specifically, doing a repeated "mental rehearsal" of their upcoming performance, race, meeting, etc.

- Real magic can unfold quite quickly, down to the details: like the royal purples in the penthouse I envisioned, or the Spotify playlist cover! Get ready for some "WOW!" moments!

- Use "quantum leaps" to combine heightened vibration and detailed visualization for rapid shifts in your life experience.

Design Your Quantum Leap

It's time to put the magic to the test. Whether you've never visualized before or you do every single day, making a customized quantum leap meditation will be fun and expansive.

Begin by picking a song that makes you feel really, really good. This could be a powerful instrumental ballad that evokes the "mind movie trailer" feeling of a main character deciding to bring all their dreams to fruition. Or a song that makes you want to get up and dance like no one's watching. Remember, the "feeling is the secret" here (thanks, Neville Goddard), so choose what feels best to YOU.

A typical song is around four minutes long, so this is going to be short, sweet, and easy to implement. In preparation, choose a few manifestations or scenes from your dream life that you'd like to spend some time with. This will guide your four-minute adventure. Find a comfortable seated or lying position, put your phone on Do Not Disturb, and ideally put on headphones. Begin by taking a few deep breaths to relax, deepen into being present, and let the thoughts and feelings of the day leading up to the moment float away like clouds. When you're ready, press play on your song choice.

Then, let your mind wander. Visit the scenes you preplanned to visit, and make them real, as if you're stepping into a memory. It should have that level of vividness. This may take some practice at first. If you struggle with visualizing images, you're not alone. Answer this question for yourself: If I told you to remember the last time you were at the beach, how would you remember it? Can you smell the sea breeze? Can you hear the crashing waves? There are ways we can "visualize" without any visual at all. However you remember a memory, that is how you should construct a future visualization. This is where make-believe really comes in handy!

In addition to playing out the manifestations you preplanned, also give your mind the space it may want to wander and add in details that may feel unexpected. This is especially fun when you're feeling really good! Let it be an unfolding process, getting to know yourself and your desires on a deeper level. Over time, you'll come to learn which scenes make you happiest to visualize, and then you can revisit those tried-and-trues during your daily quantum leaps.

REPEAT, REPEAT, REPEAT! Notice how your day feels extra sparkly after taking a few minutes to do this, and commit to the practice for the sake of the **fun** of it. Then sit back, relax, and watch the mind movie come to fruition!

CHAPTER 3

INTO THE DEPTHS OF
THE SUBCONSCIOUS MIND

I have a friend who wanted to sell his car after his girlfriend moved away. It was the car they had purchased together and driven for years of many great memories. While they hadn't broken up, he was tending to some emotional pain around the new long-distance relationship and a lot of nostalgia about how good and easy it was when they lived together. The car represented these memories to him.

When he was ready to sell the car, he got in to drive it to a prospective buyer, and noticed that suddenly, all the check engine and service lights had lit up on the dashboard. Thinking it was an unexpected issue, he canceled the meeting with the prospective buyer and instead took the car to the mechanic, who informed him that the car was fine, and the lights were a false alarm. He drove it that night with no issues and no more lights.

He then set up another appointment with a prospective buyer the next day, assured that all was well with the car. When he got into the car to drive it to the meeting . . . the exact same thing happened. All the lights came up on the dashboard. Déjà vu.

Obviously, he couldn't tell the buyer, "Don't worry, I got this all checked out yesterday and the mechanic assured me it's okay." I don't know much about buying cars, but I would advise us all not to give a stranger the benefit of the doubt if a car is displaying that many service lights! So of course, he couldn't move ahead with the meeting . . . once again.

What's the deal here? Does the car just happen to know when it's about to be sold, so it throws a fit and lights itself up on the dashboard, not wanting to part with its owner?

Upon further evaluation, the situation was crystal clear . . . and chilling. This wasn't about the car at all. This car was in impeccable condition; the mechanic himself said so. This was about my friend.

To him, selling the car felt like doubling the loss of having his girlfriend nearby. He wasn't thinking of this consciously. He was just trying to sell the car. But these emotions were right beneath the surface. To his subconscious, it felt emotionally safer to keep the car because it made him feel closer to her and the life they had together when they lived in the same city. So—how convenient!—his external reality reflected *exactly what his subconscious wanted*. The external circumstances provided the perfect excuse not to sell the car.

I get it: this story sounds almost unbelievable. How can a car respond to our thoughts, beliefs, and emotions? But by now you know that life is ALWAYS responding to our thoughts, beliefs, and emotions. And it's so much deeper than it appears at first glance.

In the first two chapters of this book, we've talked a lot about what we can do consciously to change our lives. We can move some serious mountains with the power of visualization and changing how we think. But all that promised transformation (which you may have already experienced if you've tried on some new perspectives or started visualizing!) is merely the tip of the iceberg as long as we're talking about the conscious mind. The *real* potency is underneath the surface: it's in our subconscious minds.

Your subconscious rules about 95 percent of the processing of your brain. 95 percent! That means everything we've discussed to date is only 5 percent of the equation. This is also where so many people give up, and positive thinking gets a bad rep or is hard to maintain beyond a few spirited days of *Alright, NOW is the moment I'm definitely turning my life around!*

Willing ourselves to think "Opportunity is out there!" and "Everything just works out for me!" can be incredibly difficult when our subconscious minds are processing very different information. In fact, the subconscious mind may be outright rejecting these new infused thoughts based on limiting beliefs about opportunity or emotionally potent memories from events in the past that did anything *but* "work out."

This is also where I got stuck in that swampy abyss before I learned about the Subconscious Breakthrough Formula and EFT Tapping. For as much as my new mindset and those manifesting books served me, I still had a deep trove of limiting subconscious beliefs that kept a metaphorical ceiling above my head in terms of how much I could grow, achieve, and accomplish. I needed to address what was subconscious in order to slingshot forward. My wholehearted attempts to move myself forward and keep my vibe high were destined to lose steam until I looked underneath the proverbial car hood of my own psyche. Why?

Your subconscious mind is a record of everything that has ever happened to you or around you. All of it. Remember how your brain can process only 0.0004 percent of the external stimuli around you at any given moment? That's just your CONSCIOUS mind.

Your subconscious mind is never missing a single detail.

This means everything—things you can't remember, things you can, things that were said around you, things you watched in movies, things that were modeled to you—has all been diligently recorded by your subconscious mind. And aside from this very impressive task of accumulating information, it has one other job that it takes very seriously: *the responsibility of keeping you safe.*

This is innate to the subconscious's responsibilities because of what it's in charge of! Your subconscious mind controls all your body's functions. As you've been reading, you haven't thought consciously, "Oh, shoot! I need to make sure I'm breathing!" You haven't thought consciously about needing to make your own heart beat or digest your food. If you're sitting outside basking in the sun, you haven't thought consciously about turning on some sweat to cool you off. All of this is up to the subconscious mind.

Here's an overview of everything your subconscious mind has to manage:

- **Running the Show with Your Body's Processes:** As I mentioned, your subconscious mind controls things like your heart rate, digestion, breathing, and blood pressure without you having to think about them. Which is a relief. And really shows the intelligence of the subconscious. It's running a tight ship! That's a *lot* to oversee at once.

- **Maintaining Equilibrium:** Your subconscious helps keep your body in balance by regulating things like temperature, fluids, and pH levels. It's like your body's own personal manager, making sure everything runs smoothly. When something is off, it has resources it can kick into gear to regain balance, like making sure you start to sweat when you're working out so you don't overheat.

- **Hormone Levels:** It also manages the release of hormones, which are like messengers in your body that help control things like your metabolism, growth, stress levels, and even reproduction.

- **Your Immunity:** Your subconscious plays a role in how well your immune system works. But oh, it goes deeper. Your emotions and stress levels can affect your immune system through your subconscious mind!

- **Emotional HQ:** Your subconscious is responsible for your feelings and emotions, like happiness, sadness, and fear. Sometimes you might not even understand why you're feeling a certain way—this is your subconscious at work. We will get SO into this as this book goes on. Get ready!

- **The Great Remember-er:** As I mentioned, it's responsible for storing and recalling memories, even ones you might not be aware of. These memories form belief systems and can affect our habits and choices, which leads me to . . .

• **Building Habits:** Your subconscious helps form habits—those things you do on autopilot. We can be consciously thinking of literally anything else while driving, brushing our teeth, or tying our shoelaces because our subconscious has got it covered.

• **Processing Your Environment:** Remember the example of two people on the same plane in the same row, both in window seats? Their wildly different experiences came down to a combination of their conscious AND subconscious minds. Your subconscious helps you understand the world around you by processing what you see, hear, and feel. It helps you figure out what's important and what to pay attention to. The RAS is a combination of conscious and subconscious processing—this is the other component.

So take this in for a moment: your subconscious mind has been doing *all this* your entire life without your conscious input. You did not instruct it to release your hormones or regulate your body temperature. Cue it saying, "You're not the boss of me!" This should be exciting evidence of how much has been going on *mentally* without your conscious control or acknowledgment. Peering into the subconscious is like unlocking an entire treasure trove of motivations, inhibitions, restrictions, and beliefs that you never consciously knew were there—but those subconscious faculties have been running the show this entire time, just like how they've been managing your heart rate and digestion.

You know how I've said you get what you focus on? Like how you keep seeing a yellow Jeep when you're thinking about buying one? *That effect comes from only 5 percent of your brain's functionality: the conscious mind.*

So here's the breakthrough: everything else that is showing up in your reality is a reflection of what your subconscious has accumulated and how it has processed this information. Which, until you found this book and committed to doing subconscious work, was seemingly out of your conscious control or direction.

This includes your relationships, your career, your mood, what happens in your personal life, what DOESN'T happen in your personal life. All the things that make you say, "This ALWAYS happens to me!" Whether you always seem to attract the same type of romantic partner in different fonts, or you always get passed over for promotions, or you can't seem to make a sale for the life of you. This is all reflective of what your subconscious mind believes to be true about each area of your life.

Since your subconscious's number one prerogative is keeping you safe, it wants you to keep attracting the same experiences as you HAVE BEEN EXPERIENCING. Why? It's what's familiar. It's what's predictable. We feel far more comfortable choosing to drive a car (if you know how to drive, of course) instead of choosing to fly a helicopter (if you don't know how to fly one). EVEN IF the helicopter would be a far more exciting experience and an expeditious route to your destination.

In the same way you don't know how to fly a helicopter, your subconscious doesn't know how to operate in the unknown. *All it knows is what it knows.* And so it only wants to do what it knows because that's just what's safer. In the same way that if someone said you can either take a helicopter or car to the grocery store right now, you'd be like, "I'm good with the car. Today isn't quite feeling like the day to throw myself into the wild risk of flying a helicopter with no previous knowledge or training."

The SAME is true of whatever it is we want in life. Our subconscious is saying, "I'm good with staying in this meh job. Today isn't quite feeling like the day to throw myself into the wild risk of applying for that job I REALLY want."

Or,

"I'm good with putting off filming until tomorrow. Today isn't quite feeling like the day to throw myself into the wild risk of exposing myself online for the world to see."

Or,

"I'm good staying in this holding pattern in my situationship where I don't know what exactly we are. I actually have a deep fear of commitment because I believe they'll leave me anyway, so it feels safer not to dive all the way in than to go ahead. Today isn't quite feeling like the day to get into a full-blown relationship and run the risk they'll shatter my heart into a million pieces in the future."

This is why it can be so darn hard to change our lives. We are basically losing a mental wrestling match with 95 percent of our brain. It might sound amazing to make more money or get "discovered" or fall in love with The One. But if that feels like brand-new territory to our subconscious mind, *or* it feels like it comes ridden with major dangers, it's going to get nixed every time.

The danger part of this is also fascinating. The subconscious doesn't know the difference between the "dangers" of tiptoeing on a tightrope one thousand feet above ground, getting onstage in front of a huge crowd of people, and putting yourself out there to go on another date after a devastating breakup. It processes all danger in the same way: If something makes my heart race faster and *feels* scary, it must *be* life-or-death scary. And that means we gotta pull the plug on it. It's a HARD NO for us.

That physiological reaction to getting onstage, however, also *comes from* the subconscious and its interpretation of our past experiences. Let's think this through using an example.

Imagine that someone, we'll call her Alice, is a saxophone player and is scouted for an exciting opportunity to play with a band at a popular jazz club in New York City. It's everything she has been consciously wanting: It's a great exposure opportunity, she gets to meet other musicians, and the gig pays pretty well, too. So, she says YES!—and immediately feels some butterflies in her stomach. And it's not a good feeling. More like . . . bats in her stomach.

"Hmm," she thinks to herself. "That's weird! This seems like such a great opportunity, but I feel so nervous."

As the evening of the performance draws closer, her nerves only continue to rise. She has a few nightmares about it going badly. She feels her heartbeat quicken whenever she gets a message about it. Her best friend is so excited to come watch her from the audience, but Alice starts to insist, "Please, no! I'll just tell you about it after. I'd rather there be one less person in the audience."

What is going on here? And why is it so darn relatable?

This is Alice's subconscious mind doing some top-notch bodyguard work. Her conscious mind would prefer to be cool and collected about this opportunity. In an ideal world, she would only feel excitement and focus. She could look forward to this performance in the same way she looks forward to a vacation. She could feel calm in the lead up, and in her power onstage. But this is just not happening, and it's not her conscious mind that's to blame.

Her subconscious is coming to the table in the boardroom of Alice's psyche with some INFORMATION. This information is a blend of everything she's ever heard, seen, or experienced when it comes to getting up in front of groups of people. Even if she has never performed at a jazz club. Even if she has never played saxophone for more people than her saxophone instructor and sometimes her cat. Something in this blend is causing the fear. But what?

Perhaps there is one very, very vital piece of information that we're missing. This is a MAJOR deal, so hold on to your seat.

Maybe there was a time in first grade when Alice had to give a presentation in front of her classroom. She was just getting over a cold that day and was sounding nasally. As she started talking, she noticed a few kids in the class snickering about her nasal tone. "You sound like Rudolph!" laughed one of the boys in the back.

"Quiet down, class!" the teacher scolded. Taking a big deep breath, Alice continued on. In the middle of the final sentence, in the home run of the entire operation, she suddenly felt like she was going to sneeze. But she didn't. Instead, she was suspended in that awkward, eyes half-closed half sneeze for what felt like fifteen minutes. When she finally sneezed, she sneezed with such force that it made a honking sound, akin to a duck quacking into a megaphone. The entire class ERUPTED with laughter, and she went back to her seat, face beet red from embarrassment.

You betcha that her subconscious mind recorded that experience DILIGENTLY. Anything that is accompanied by a strong negative emotion gets written in red ink all over your subconscious. It grades it and marks it to never, ever forget: Danger! Danger! Danger!

Her subconscious mind interpreted the situation as "Getting up in front of others to share my work results in humiliation and embarrassment. Therefore, it is a risk to my safety."

For better or worse, your subconscious mind is biologically rigged to make sure you are accepted by your community. Remember, for so much of human history, community = survival. People lived together in groups and depended on one another for food, shelter, and resources. "Getting voted off the island" was essentially a death sentence, so acceptance by the community was necessary.

This is also why it can feel so emotionally distressing to hear that someone doesn't like you, or to experience a form of rejection. We'll get to this more later, but for the sake of Alice's story, this sneezing experience was Bad News. And her subconscious filed it under "experiences to avoid at all costs."

Now, it's several decades later, she's a talented saxophone player, she doesn't have a cold, there's no presentation, no classroom, and she's even in a different city. And yet, her subconscious has scanned its history of Everything That Has Ever Happened that could be loosely related to this impending saxophone performance, has found the Classroom Sneeze Disaster memory, and is thinking, "UH OH. Red ink. Red ink! RED INK! THIS IS VERY, VERY BAD."

So it is sounding some major alarm bells. Hence the bad dreams, and the butterfly-bats, and the increasing anxiety as the day of the performance draws closer. Depending on the intensity of the fear (which really, is just about the number of related "red ink: DANGER!" files), she might self-sabotage. Perhaps she becomes convinced that the energy of the performance was simply not right, so she ends up canceling to feel some relief—even though there's also a slight feeling of discomfort or disappointment following this decision, like her soul wondering what could have been if she had just been brave. Perhaps the stress weakens her immune system and she gets a cold that renders her unable to show up and perform, which would be some REAL subconscious prophecy-fulfilling. Perhaps her train into the city the day of the performance gets canceled, which she then takes as a very convenient sign that she was not supposed to perform. Perhaps the show gets canceled because of a problem at the venue. A blizzard blows through. Her saxophone goes missing.

The subconscious mind has very, very interesting ways of protecting us. And until we figure out *why* it's so intent on protecting us, then clear the Red Ink file from the root, we're powerless to stop it. It will just feel like an odd—and very *convenient*—coincidence.

One thing's for sure: as you continue to read this book and read more true stories from the lives of my friends, my clients, my community, and my own life, you'll start to see that something magical is happening. And that maybe—just maybe—reality is a projection of what's going on in our subconscious minds.

How do we change reality? We dive deeper. We dive into the subconscious and change it from there.

Perception vs. Reality

Part of understanding how the subconscious rules everything is understanding that sometimes perception and reality are very, very different things. What constitutes your personal reality is never the entire story because, again, your reticular activating system can take in and perceive only 0.0004 percent of everything happening around you based on what it deems to be relevant to you. Additionally, your subconscious is making snap judgments and piecing together "evidence" at a speed faster than your conscious mind can comprehend to create your reactions to the world around you. You're not consciously sorting through the information, deciding for yourself what is and isn't relevant or useful. It's a full-blown operation happening unconsciously.

This could mean that the partner of your dreams once bumped their shopping cart into yours at the grocery store by accident and said, "Oops, sorry!" but before you could look up and make eye contact, your subconscious processed, in less than a split second, the following information . . .

"Oh my, okay, it's happening, a potential partner, straight out of our dreams, WOW helllllllooo, can you say GORGEOUS? Let's shut it down! We simply cannot do this because last time we opened ourselves up to the L word we were BETRAYED, plus our full focus should be on work right now, and dating is always such a distraction, so let's just wipe out this tiny, now inconsequential piece of evidence that we bumped shopping carts with this angelic human, irrelevant, thank you, next!"

Your conscious mind had no idea this was happening or that this domino effect of "OH NO! WE COULD BE HEADING TOWARD AN EMOTIONAL DISASTER!" was unfolding in your panicked subconscious mind. You likely smiled politely, half-distracted, and thought to yourself, "Okay, where's the tomato paste?"

The Cause of Differing Opinions

This is the same reason that your reaction to everything is unique to YOU—it's YOUR perception. This is why so many people have wildly differing opinions on movies, books, and celebrities. The celebrity you idolize and adore is another's archnemesis (even though they've never met)—their voice is screechy, their laugh is annoying, they seem so stuck up, etc. Does this make this celebrity "bad" or "good"? No—they're just being perceived by the public, and everyone's perception of them will be different because it has basically nothing to do with the actual celebrity. *Perception isn't reality. But our perception of something makes it **our** experienced reality.*

It's the same for your favorite song, book, or movie. The piece of art that brought you to tears, that you feel perfectly encapsulates your life, that changed your entire reason for existing and rocket-launched you to a whole new stratosphere—for another person, that song, book, or movie was the worst thing they've ever consumed, and they wish they could get that time back. Perception. So, what is reality? How can we really say with absolute certainty what IS or ISN'T true?

Which leads me to one of the most important takeaways from this book, that will alter the entire course of your life:

Only YOU can decide what is true for you.

Just because you believe something doesn't make it "true" in absolute terms. However, YOUR BELIEF IN IT MAKES IT TRUE *FOR YOU*. You cannot see what you do not believe you *can* see. It can be smack in front of your face, but if you don't believe it's possible or true, it's as if it's invisible. Your reticular activating system and subconscious mind can only look for and locate in reality what is ALREADY within you. What you *expect* to see, and what you have *trained* yourself to see.

A powerful example of this is what we know as the placebo effect. This is when doctors administer "sugar pills" or other "fake" types of medicine but tell the patient that the prescriptions are actual, effective medications with active ingredients that will relieve their symptoms. Despite the absence of the active ingredient that would lead to healing, the patient's belief in the medication causes an observable shift.

Dr. Henry Beecher's groundbreaking paper titled "The Powerful Placebo" was published in the *Journal of the American Medical Association* in 1955. In this influential study, Beecher reviewed fifteen clinical trials from his own experiences as a physician during World War II across several types of medical conditions, ranging from the common cold to pectoral angina.

Beecher found that in these trials, a surprisingly high proportion of patients experienced symptom relief or improvement after receiving an inactive treatment (placebo) instead of an actual medication. Specifically, he noted that approximately 35 percent of patients across the trials showed positive responses to the placebo treatment, reporting reduced pain or improved symptoms.

So we know that the mind is where we hold great power. Our beliefs inform our experience. Your perception of the world and your place in it truly creates your entire experience in this life. What you believe can help you experience something *positively*. The ramifications of this create the pillars of this book, which is why the subconscious mind is so critically important. You may consciously think you believe something, like "I deserve to be wealthy," but if you're experiencing something very, very different, the subconscious mind is the place to look.

This is, in my humble opinion, one of the most exciting parts of life. Because what if all the *negative* perceptions you've carried with you could be proven false through a shift in your belief system? What if you could find and eliminate the sneaky subconscious beliefs that have been keeping you stuck?

What if you could begin to see—and therefore experience—everything in your reality as lucky, fortuitous, and on your side?

What if your career could feel easy and natural, like walking on stars, with all your dreams coming true and new ideas striking every day?

What if your relationships could always be incredibly easy, deep, and fulfilling, featuring romantic strolls by the water and deep belly laughs over cucumber spritzers with new best friends?

What if your abundance could surge until you're making it RAIN, while you also feel deeply secure and more on top of your money management than ever?

Fill in the blank with the WHAT IF of your dreams.

What then?

Subconscious Breakthrough File

Margaret, a member of my Dreamaway community, was struggling with the belief that money is hard to make. This is a highly common one (raise your hand if you currently are being, or have EVER been, personally victimized by this exact limiting belief)—and the more common a belief system is, the more likely it is that it's deeply rooted, because it's been affirmed by people around us time and time again. Margaret didn't trust herself with large sums of money.

"My subconscious believed I would always spend more than what I brought in, so why bother with allowing money in anyways?" she reflected.

So, the beliefs were tied together: "Money is hard to make, and that's fine, because if I were to easily make lots of money, I'd just spend it all."

(This is frequently how it happens. We always have multiple beliefs around areas of our lives, and the beliefs create "knots" tangled up with one another. If you'd like, review the statements you came up with about each area of your life during the Habitual Thought exercise back in chapter 1 and see how the stories and core beliefs intertwine for you!)

Margaret had PLENTY of evidence for this belief system. Her family had always teased her about being bad with money, and then she had accumulated lots of debt in college that she had trouble paying off.

These beliefs were especially detrimental because it was her dream to scale a thriving coaching business alongside her job. The goal: to call in high-ticket clients who would happily purchase her coaching plan. She refined her marketing and messaging for this goal and felt confident in *what* she was selling and the value she knew she was offering . . . but it was absolute crickets for a while. Not a single sale.

When she dug deeper into her subconscious mind to figure out the stuckness, she quickly realized why she was experiencing this. It was twofold. She didn't believe it could be that easy to make that much money,

AND she didn't think she could handle making those larger sums from higher-paying clients.

Because she believed it, it continued to be true for her. It was hard to make money. And she remained unable to land a high-ticket client ...

... until she shifted her belief system on money. She used one of my courses that relied on tapping (stay tuned—you'll be learning more about this very soon!) called "Made for More" to establish security and new beliefs around receiving MORE money ...

... and within THAT WEEK, she signed her first high-ticket coaching client, got a raise at work, AND received a bonus she was not expecting at all.

If you're wondering, HOW CAN IT BE THAT EASY? I get it—I've been doing this work for a long, long time, and reading these stories still makes my jaw drop to the floor like I'm in one of those cartoons. But it's just more evidence that we get what we believe, and we can rewire our belief systems in very little time. And once there's a new belief system integrated, it's just a matter of time until it's reflected in the external world.

"But I don't get it, Haley," I can imagine you saying. "How did her shifted belief system in being able to call in a client *actually* call in a client who purchased from her? How could her belief change another person's behavior?"

This one's up to personal belief, depending how woo-woo you want to get. I see two options here and have experienced a little of both.

1. It's totally possible that she had clients interested and sending inquiring emails or messages, but she quite literally did not see this communication because she didn't believe it could be that easy and she didn't believe she could handle it.

A personal story here: I'll never forget the time that I shared a video on my music Instagram of me performing a song I'd just written. I loved this song and thought the video was a great take of me singing and playing the piano. At this time, I was really struggling with the belief system "Very few people care about my music." Honestly, it was closer to "*No one* cares about my music," but I had a few reliable followers who were expressing their support on my then-small music Instagram.

This was one of those songs that totally thrilled me to write—I was obsessed with it from the get-go and could barely fall asleep that night out of sheer excitement. I had just posted it on my Instagram story, and I was sure I'd receive some replies from others who felt the same about the song. The next morning, I had maybe two messages. I immediately felt discouraged. Was I crazy? Was this song not actually good at all? All the old thoughts and patterns of self-doubt started to flood back in.

And the thing about self-doubt is it comes with friends! It likes to hit ya with all the related belief systems. "Maybe I'm not meant for this. I keep trying and no one seems to care or notice. I should just stop. This is embarrassing at this rate. I obviously can't trust what I think is a good song or performance."

Luckily, I had an EFT Tapping session (again, you'll be learning ALL about this soon!) with one of my coaches that morning and we worked through some of these feelings—stopping them in their tracks, tracing them back to their root cause, and clearing them for good. I felt a noticeable shift by the end of the session, and I got some of my encouragement back. I chose to make the whole situation a WIN—I was definitely expanding as a songwriter, and this song was proof of that on a purely personal level! With renewed confidence, I pulled up the app again to really take a moment with the couple sweet messages I *had* gotten.

As I opened my inbox, my eyes widened. There they were—TONS of other replies to my song! They'd been received throughout the night beginning right after I posted. I couldn't believe my eyes. How had I not seen these?! I had checked my message requests more times than I'd like to admit in print.

The messages felt like presents on Christmas morning. Each one validated exactly what I felt about the song. Someone said they believed it represented my songwriting reaching a whole new league. Someone else asked me to please finish the song as soon as possible because she wanted it to be her WEDDING song!

As excited as I was, I was also puzzled. I'd been in such distress and self-doubt because of the lack of response to the song . . . which wasn't even true. But yet again, because I believed it, it made it TRUE for ME. With what I know about the subconscious, the only rational explanation is that my eyes literally filtered out the fact I had message requests. Which makes me want to get my vision checked. But that's how it works! WE CANNOT SEE WHAT WE DON'T BELIEVE.

The same may have happened with Margaret as well.

Onto the second theory, which is a bit more woo-woo:

2. It's totally possible that we actually have infinite potential realities in front of us at any moment—*and we are navigating them through our energy and beliefs.*

Remember how I said that I believed that I was "receiving a vision" of a penthouse suite that already existed in all my visualizations? Despite my belief in my own magic, I don't totally buy that my mind fully constructed a space that hadn't been built yet and that space just happened to materialize on the top floor of a hotel that was a few avenues away from me at the time.

Many quantum physicists are big believers that this one reality is not all there is, and that we can actually move into "different realities" all the time. This never happens in blatant ways—you're never going to open your eyes after a meditation and realize you're in a totally different room, for example. This isn't a sci-fi movie. But you will notice subtle differences where things just "feel" a bit different, and serendipitous happenings begin to occur—and in this type of subconscious uncovering and rewiring work, there will also eventually be big differences by way of what you're attracting into your reality.

According to this theory, there are infinite potential realities that are all slightly different—but the further you get from this one via your energetic choices and belief system shifts, the more you'll actually notice the differences. As another example, remember the hypotheticals I presented in chapter 1 about two ways to spend the same evening, the first in the ex-stalking, thriller-watching frenzy, and the other in the peace-encouraging, deeply rested, humming-along-to-your-favorite-tune sailboat? Depending on your choices, you can open to different possibilities for the exact same day because your mood and point of focus change what you see and what you experience (thanks to our friend the RAS).

The RAS isn't just tied up with our conscious thoughts and point of focus. The subconscious has a major part to play! Whatever your subconscious believes is what it's going to get more of—which is why, when you change the core belief, reality shifts. It doesn't resonate with me that shifting realities is like changing channels on a television; rather, there's a broadening of perspective to see what's always been there, just under our noses, but hiding in plain sight until we could guide our subconscious minds to register it. That 0.0004 percent of reality that we perceive in any given moment shifts a bit, to include more evidence of the new belief and less of the old one.

I will say, that doesn't *totally* explain a lot of the magic I've witnessed and experienced, but it's a start. Is magic meant to be "figured out," or can we sit back in appreciation of it, noticing what works and continuing forward to unlock even more magic?

A lot of this is theoretical, based on continuing stacks of evidence from my life and the lives of my friends and clients. The pattern goes as follows:

The individual goes within and identifies the negative belief system that has been keeping them stuck.

They then shift and clear the belief and accompanying emotions utilizing EFT Tapping.

They feel noticeably better, in a space of empowerment and motivation, or simply more peace.

And within weeks, they experience a corresponding shift in their reality, which frequently is more like MASSIVE leaps—like Margaret getting a raise and a bonus the same week as the client booking.

When I first began creating content online, I had some funky beliefs.

An overview of a few of them:

• What I have to say isn't that interesting or entertaining.

• It isn't safe to post because people from my past will see and laugh at me.

• It's really hard to attract viewers and build an audience.

• The more SEEN I am, the less safe I am.

• I need to work really, really hard to be successful and get views, followers, and exposure.

Those are just the ones I remember! Another cool part of rewiring beliefs is that you'll get a bit of belief amnesia. They just won't be relevant or ring true anymore . . . so you'll forget them!

Before I started my deep dive into these subconscious beliefs, I thought the way to social media success was through strategy alone. I'd spend so much time refining the captions on my content it was as if I thought they had to be the next great American novel. If I got a fraction more engagement than usual, I'd double down with increasing desperation. It was such a frustrating time, like moving with all my might through thick molasses, barely making it an inch when my effort should've propelled me into a new zip code.

Attracting an audience was number one on my goal list, so it became a priority to work on during EFT sessions. The more I went within and discovered the belief systems holding me back, the more "ohhhh, NO WONDER!" moments I had, and the more I cleared.

It only took a little bit. Easily and naturally, I started to experience something brand new:

1. I'd get a spark of a new idea for a video that felt fun and playful.

2. I'd do it ASAP, and I really enjoyed it—it was very easy and flowed off my tongue.

3. Once I'd post, it would immediately take off, frequently accumulating hundreds of thousands of views.

The first time it happened, I couldn't believe my eyes. My audience was growing exponentially—for a video that came completely naturally! And I'd been putting in a marathon and circus of effort beforehand, all for CRICKETS?

This is where I *do* believe that we can shift timelines into new realms of possibility that reflect our new belief systems, including what we believe is safe for us and what's in alignment with our perceived identity. It was not until I believed it was safe to be seen and saw myself as someone who could be seen by the masses that I experienced it. Before this, it just did not matter how *much* I wanted it. How *hard* I worked for it. I was always going to be trudging through the molasses, barely making progress, until I figured out why my subconscious was putting up such a fight.

Which leads me to another part of this book that will change your entire life if you really hear me here:

Unless all of you—conscious mind and subconscious mind—is 100 percent on board with what you want, it isn't going to happen.

Let's turn it into a math formula to make it fun. (Math? Fun? I know, but stay with me.)

Conscious desire to build a following + subconscious fear of being seen by more than ten people = Not going to happen.

Conscious desire to become an award-winning actress on the silver screen + subconscious fear that you're actually not talented enough for it = Not going to happen.

Conscious desire to make big money with your business + subconscious fear you'll just lose it all = Not going to happen.

Conscious desire to find and buy your dream home + subconscious fear you can't handle that at this stage of your life = Not going to happen.

BUT YOU ARE NOT STUCK. *You* have the magic, remember?

NO ONE is in charge of your subconscious beliefs but YOU.

At ANY TIME, you can reverse the limiting belief, clear the block, and experience a vastly different reality.

Conscious desire to build a following + subconscious comfortable with it, too = Inevitable.

Conscious desire to become an award-winning actress + subconscious confidence in your skills = Inevitable.

Conscious desire to make big money with your business + subconscious belief that it will be easy and stable = Inevitable.

Conscious desire to buy your dream home + subconscious readiness to nest in that space = Inevitable.

Subconscious Breakthrough File

Sometimes, the subconscious has sneaky reasons for not wanting to succeed that have little to do with the actual success. One of my clients came to me because she was trying to start scaling her freelance writing efforts but found that she was majorly struggling with productivity. She just couldn't bring herself to sit down and get the work done, even with looming deadlines. She started giving her clients excuses, usually related to health issues, but didn't understand why she couldn't get a grip on this. She saw how it was sabotaging her efforts to build a business and make money.

"It just felt like a constant drag to have all that work looming over me," she shared in hindsight.

As we peeled back the layers of it, we realized it was a pattern from childhood. Because she had undergone a few health issues while growing up, she was commonly able to use "I don't feel well" as an excuse to miss school and extend deadlines. She had come to really like this freedom and found herself using it even when she felt completely fine. Now, she saw how it was hurting her relationships with her clients, and we unpacked together that her subconscious was trying to keep her safe from scaling her business.

To her subconscious mind, delivering on time for clients = the ability to deliver on time for MORE clients = taking on an increasing workload with more deadlines to deliver on time for = total loss of freedom.

Once we found this and rewired it to what she would rather believe, everything shifted. It served her MORE to believe that scaling her business could actually help her freedom! And maybe getting the work done could be a breeze that she would knock out first thing in the morning and even look forward to. We combined EFT Tapping and visualization to achieve this rewire.

Within weeks, getting client work done on time became an easy, satisfying experience for her, and her business has only continued to scale ever since—and she's proven to herself she can handle big projects like a boss! She's experiencing even more freedom, joy, and ease than she ever knew. It turns out she didn't need the excuses and lack of productivity to be safe.

"I haven't had that feeling that things are a drag in the slightest in probably a full year . . . and my prices are about four times what they were and I'm doing work that's objectively higher-stakes and more complicated to get right!" she shared with me when we caught up. "I used to think 'what if it could all just be easy and you could look forward to the work' was kind of a pipe dream, but I really, truly feel that way about running my business now."

More safety AND more joy were right around the corner for her, just a change in belief away.

Changing Your Beliefs

As we'll get into in part 2, I believe one of the most powerful ways to shift your subconscious beliefs is via EFT Tapping to release the old belief, as well as other forms of subconscious work. However, while we're still in the warmup, here are some tips to start to get your mind going toward a brand-new story. Don't underestimate these exercises, because you'll use them forever and ever, even with your new subconscious breakthrough toolbox. People have been changing their belief systems for many a century without the Subconscious Breakthrough Formula and EFT. Just because I've found a rapid and fun way to change your life doesn't mean there aren't many other ways you can access your inherent magic.

It's important to know that you didn't get your beliefs out of thin air. Every single one of your beliefs is held together in your brain by a cluster of associated memories and relevant information, originating somewhere, at some point, whether from something someone told you, something you observed, or something you experienced. You can imagine that every belief in your brain is a filing folder of relevant information that brought your subconscious mind to this conclusion.

It's pretty basic, really. If you believe the sky is blue, it's because someone told you it is, and then you saw a blue sky quite literally hundreds of thousands of times. Each time this happened, it confirmed the original statement—"the sky is blue"—with evidence. "Oh, look at that, it IS blue!" your subconscious thought to itself as it diligently recorded the evidence.

Now, later in your life, that's one THICK filing folder of proof for this sky color belief! If someone asked you to PROVE the sky is blue, you could pull out evidence from every single day of your life that you looked at the sky and every single time someone referenced the sky being blue. Of course, this would be your SUBCONSCIOUS coming to defend you and prove this belief system like a great attorney. You don't consciously remember every single bit of evidence from every single time you ever looked at the sky and it was blue—and good thing, because it would be getting crowded up in your brain. All you know is you consciously believe it and you have plenty of conscious evidence for it on top of the nearly infinite subconscious evidence.

But because your subconscious remembers everything and you consciously DON'T, things get interesting when we look at more insidious beliefs. Your subconscious has beliefs you aren't even consciously aware of, because it's remembering evidence that you don't consciously remember. How do you know what you believe? It is mirrored in what's showing up in your reality. Plus, you're about to delve into some groundbreaking subconscious breakthrough questions that will help you unlock that unconscious treasure chest and reveal an abundance of "aha" moments that will quite literally explain everything that's been happening in your life.

Confirmation Bias, Subconscious Edition

Additionally, all it takes is your subconscious mind's successful installation of a belief system to ensure that belief file will attract more evidence and data left and right. Remember: your reticular activating system is only taking in what it believes is *relevant*. If you *believe* something, your reticular activating system is incredible at sniffing out anything that remotely resembles evidence of a belief system. Even if it's not real evidence! It will alter your perception of reality to fit the bill of a belief you already have, because that's actually just more energy efficient for the brain.

Remember how I couldn't see the many affirming messages in my message requests folder, because I believed people didn't care? This was actually more energy efficient for my brain, which is processing information faster than any of us can imagine. This isn't a slow, deliberate choice in the boardroom of our brains like in the movie *Inside Out*. This is a split-second evaluation of reality, sifting information according to what belief systems are being experienced. The brain will arrive at a conclusion based on what makes the most sense to it—which always favors whichever belief filing folder is the thickest and most packed with information. I like to think of these thick filing folders as "stories." When they're the most-used and most-referenced folders, the subconscious keeps it close by and assigns a story to it. In my case, it was the story that "No one cares about my music."

Perhaps you've experienced this in a disagreement with a friend, or a time when you two felt off with each other. Maybe they were going through a hard time and pulled back from you in a way you noticed. It wasn't about you at all, but suddenly your brain went into Story Mode from past painful experiences in relationships. Now, the story is getting really elaborate and dramatic and detailed. Their change in behavior reveals your own insecurities—"do they even want to be my friend?" or "I feel like they're mad that I had to reschedule our walk last week!"

Meanwhile, imagine your friend isn't thinking about you negatively at all, they're just turtle-shelling to work through some personal growth opportunities. Your brain launched off into a spiral on its own—but not out of thin air! It was calling on an internally stored evidence folder of friendship wounds, because it felt relevant.

Input: Friend pulling away.

Relevant file folder: Friends pull away when they're mad and don't want to be friends anymore.

Evidence: Multiple ex-friends who pulled away and eventually ghosted.

Reaction: Potential feelings of sadness, shame, anger, and "why does this always happen in my friendships?" and potential behaviors like stonewalling (retreating into your own turtle shell and going cold) or asking the friend incessantly if anything is wrong.

The Truth: The friendship is great and thriving. The friend is on an internal journey. They'll be back to normal in a few weeks and share what they learned and what they were going through.

In the case of this example, your reaction is actually about you, not your friend. Even though it feels like your friend is doing something to you, their behavior is simply bringing out a deeper wound and limiting belief within you from past friendship experiences.

Someone else may experience the exact same thing with that friend and be in complete peace about it the entire time, thinking to themselves, "Oh, maybe they're going through a hard time! I'll send another check-in text next week and see if I can help," and then going on with their day without any internalization of the situation.

Your reaction in this case doesn't mean anything is wrong with you or that you're dramatic, prone to making up stories, or overly reactionary. It simply means that your subconscious is looking for potential experiences of danger (which includes emotional hurt) because of past events and beliefs about friendship. Your subconscious wants to make sure nothing needs "fixing," so it won't let the matter rest until the situation is resolved—even if that resolution isn't what's actually best for you (e.g., pushing the friend away first before they can do it to you).

Understanding that others may respond and assume something completely different about the same input is a great way to start to rewire your beliefs. Ask yourself:

"If I was in a space of peace about this and *not* taking it personally, what could I see may be happening instead?"

"If I had a totally different belief system and self-perception, could I perceive this situation any differently?"

Belief in Concepts and Ways of the World

Beyond interpersonal relationships and subjective experiences, we've also built in strong neural pathways (file folders) for key concepts that are (allegedly) universally accepted.

Let's take the common belief in the "starving artist" and break it down from this perspective.

If we were to unpack and review the subconscious filing folder of a random individual who believes in the "starving artist" concept, or the idea that people who pursue creative paths will struggle, here are a few pieces of evidence we'd find:

• The fact their dad frequently said it in front of them when young

• A teacher mentioned it in passing

• Several movies, TV shows, books, or other popular media sources appealing to the same idea

• That, ahem, very encouraging cliché: "don't quit your day job"

• A few friends or relatives who pursued an artistic career and couldn't "make it"

• A few friends or relatives who are TRYING to pursue an artistic career and never seem to have much money

• Someone who told them most aspiring actresses in Hollywood and songwriters in Nashville are servers

Somewhere in the midst of all this "evidence," the belief became so ingrained that our conscious awareness skimmed right past any evidence to the contrary. There's no telling where that was, but my best bet is it was right after a parent or a teacher said it or modeled it to them. Especially in their early childhood. Up until age seven, we are only operating in a theta brainwave state, which means our subconscious minds are wide open to take in everything that is said to us and everything that happens around us as truth without any critical thinking happening.

So, after this belief became ingrained, it wouldn't matter if this same individual also had another friend who ended up selling a painting for $10 million. They'd still believe in the trope of the starving artist. And when asked about the friend who was an exception, they'd say, "Well they got lucky." Or, "They're just really talented; most artists aren't." Or, "Well they don't have a family life. Work is their life. They only made it because they work themselves to the bone." . . . or any other potential excuse. It's incredibly easy to excuse a piece of evidence that goes against our belief system. We'll call that an anomaly and fit it nice and neatly inside *another* limiting belief system filing folder like, "You have to sacrifice family to be successful" or "Most artists aren't talented."

Subconscious Breakthrough File

I had the pleasure of working with an amazing client named Salima, who had a big dream of becoming a famous author and screenwriter. However, she was battling a deep belief that she wasn't good enough to accomplish either of these goals. As a result, the prospect of a career in writing seemed wildly impossible, and her reality was reflecting that.

In our sessions, I kept asking her for positive evidence. Did she have any evidence at all that she was actually a good writer?

She did. Her dad had complimented her writing once, and a professor had given her glowing remarks. It then became an evidence game—neutralizing the emotional potency of the old evidence and fluffing up the potency (and, frankly, existence) of the positive evidence. The thing is, there's ALWAYS positive evidence. Even though our brains are unreliable narrators and show preferential treatment to the thicker file folders, they can still remember other bits and pieces of information on some level, too. More on this later.

It was an uphill battle at first—it always is, when we're overhauling belief systems. For Salima, her file folder for the belief that she wasn't a good enough writer had become SO thick that it was really challenging to imagine the contrary.

And there was a connected file folder belief system (there usually is!) that it would be way too late in her life to shift careers, that it simply wasn't realistic. She had already spent years building her marketing career and was at an age where people were starting to ask "When are you building a family?" instead of "What's your next professional move?" But her heart carried her forward; she continued to feel the burning desire to be a writer despite these limiting beliefs, and that, my friend, is the power of a dream.

Slowly but surely, her point of focus shifted to a new belief system that she IS a good writer and she CAN do this as her career. And half a year after we began working together, she was admitted to the top MFA program she applied to (and her first choice!), UCLA's MFA program in screenwriting.

How Do You KNOW?

To change our belief systems, we first must know what we're dealing with. Which leads us to the magical question "How do you KNOW?" (Really, better put, this should be "How do you BELIEVE?"—but we do take on our beliefs as knowledge even if they are not the absolute truth.)

This works for any belief. Survey your life. Pick anything—examples could be "I don't believe I can start a business that could scale to $1 million" or "I don't believe I'll ever move out of my hometown."

HOW DO YOU KNOW? Let's get into it:

1. Jot all of it down. Everything that comes to mind. None of it is "wrong." In fact, all of it is "RIGHT" for you until we look under the proverbial car hood and figure out where it's coming from and how we can shift it. This list will look a lot like the starving artist example. Who have you seen model this to you? What have you heard? Read? Seen? What has happened to you in your personal experience that proves this belief?

This is commonly one of the most fascinating parts. You'll realize you've been holding on to some wacky evidence. It's like cleaning out that one random junk drawer that's been a catch-all for every trinket and loose slip of paper you've ever lost. One time, I traced one of my limiting beliefs back to a completely fictional book I'd read in middle school. How did I know I knew that? Because somehow, the title and the premise of the book came to mind as I challenged myself on the belief. As I pieced it together, I realized that the content of the book WAS related to the belief I was unpacking! And included substantial evidence for it, too! Again, a FICTIONAL book. I'm glad I rewired that one out of there!

2. For every single piece of evidence, begin to poke around with a playful curiosity. Are we SURE this is a piece of evidence we could hold up in a court of law? In other words, is it really true? Put your subconscious on trial in advance. Go on, do it. It's decided to create a whole narrative out of these pieces of evidence ... so give it some questioning. Is it possible things could be ANY OTHER WAY?

Related to this question, the reason I ask is because of a chilling story. One of my friend's greatest pieces of "evidence" she had that she was "not worthy" came from her high school boyfriend. He was extremely hot and cold and, frankly, emotionally abusive. He would change his mind about her all the time, lie about her constantly, and pressure her to keep their relationship a secret. But he had dated other girls publicly and seemed to praise them and act consistent with them, leading her to believe that it was just something wrong with *her*, and if only she had been worthy enough, he would've treated her well, too.

Because she was so young and had deep feelings for him, this came with an extra punch, and the evidence kept evidence-ing. It didn't help that he was popular and very well-liked, making her feel like she was always on the outside, missing something or not worthy enough to be included in his circle or even just loved by him.

This haunted her for years after high school, even in his absence. It affected her perception of worthiness in relationships, of course, but it also bled over into every aspect of her life, like her career. She had so much evidence for the story that it was about her, not about him, because this pattern seemed to be exclusively the way he treated her. Then, she ended up having a chance encounter with one of his high school friends. They got to talking, and she asked in passing if he still kept in touch with her ex.

"Absolutely not," he replied, looking visibly uncomfortable.

"Oh?" she asked, raising an eyebrow.

"Did no one tell you ... ?" he started, and she shook her head, confused.

He proceeded to tell her that several of their friends had separately and distinctly experienced abuse from him.

She was beyond bewildered. All this time, she believed it was something wrong with her that was making him act this way—after all, he had so many friends who loved and adored him. Meanwhile, he was also being abusive to other people, just not in ways she could see or discern. It dawned on her that, actually, the repeated rejection was a blessing and protection. The heartbreak never meant anything about her; that was her misunderstanding. And she would've kept believing it was all about her if it wasn't for this fated conversation.

I understand not everyone has the privilege of unveiling the "truth" about pieces of evidence we've interpreted a certain way—especially not a bombshell like that, many years after the fact! But it is worth some curiosity. Try on a detective's hat and perspective: "In what way could this actually have been false?"

Some examples:

EVIDENCE: "My dad always says that pursuing a creative career leads to becoming a starving artist."

POTENTIAL CONTRARY EVIDENCE: What if that's a belief he adopted from someone else . . . who got it from someone else . . . who got it from someone else . . . and it's never actually even been true? And I've just accepted it as evidence because he told me when I was young?

EVIDENCE: "I tried to sell a script I wrote once. It didn't get off the ground at all. No interest."

POTENTIAL CONTRARY EVIDENCE: What if your subconscious just didn't believe it was possible, so you quite literally didn't see an email of interest, or your subconscious pulled a fast one on ya and you made a typo in your email address when you submitted the query forms?

EVIDENCE: "Aunt Jane is a singer and she never has any money."

POTENTIAL CONTRARY EVIDENCE: Maybe Aunt Jane makes $15,000 a gig but actually spends that much in a day on a secret designer purse addiction, and she only says she makes nothing because that's easier than admitting she has a major spending problem?

The potential contrary evidence can be as silly or as deep or as speculative as you please. It really doesn't matter. As long as it's supporting a new and more empowering story, you can take some major creative liberties. Because it's more than likely that the meaning you've derived from the evidence you *do* have is itself a bit off base, or downright silly and ridiculous.

3. Begin the hunt for positive evidence.

Now that your brain is loosey goosey from that fun, creative assignment, it's time to look for evidence to the contrary! You may believe you have none, but if you tell your subconscious to look for it, you may just start to see it. Another thing I've experienced and witnessed multiple times is the remembering of past evidence as a result of tapping—almost like it was always there, buried underneath the thick filing folder of negative belief evidence.

Again, visualization helps with this. For every belief you're rewiring, simply asking yourself, "What would I rather believe?" can lead to some major insights. A note here: Make sure what you'd rather believe is the *affirmative* of something.

So, if you're working on your belief that work will always lead to burnout, of course you'd rather believe that your work will NOT lead to burnout. But this is still a negative statement. Rather, challenge yourself to find the opposite. What is the opposite of burnout? What might you experience instead?

A new belief could be "Work gives me energy. It feels easy and fun. I have a great work-life balance, and I feel lit up by my entire career!" Wow, now how does *that* feel in comparison to "It doesn't give me burnout"?

These affirmative statements also give you direction on what to visualize. You can now start to create mind movies of you experiencing an energy boost at work. What could it feel like and look like if it was easy and fun? How would you know you have a great work-life balance? What would you tell a friend over a catch-up dinner about how much work has been lighting you up lately?

Again, it will feel like you're making it up, off in make-believe dreamland. Oh well. We had it right as kids. Do it anyway. Replay the new mind movie at least three times a day, adding more specificity and emotion every single time.

Then, in your exterior reality, you'll start to look for evidence by intentionally seeking out examples of real people who experience ease, fun, and an energy boost in their career. Even if you don't know them! This could be a celebrity or an idol. They're still evidence! At the beginning, it's going to feel like going on an Easter egg hunt because the evidence *will* be hidden. But a combination of visualizing that it could be true for you and having the intention to find it will lead to more and more evidence.

Pro tip: Make a note in your phone or somewhere readily accessible titled "New Belief Evidence." Write the belief as an affirmation at the top of the page, then fill in all the evidence you find as it reveals itself to you. What you focus on expands; this will build momentum to keep you finding more and more and more and more evidence. And before you know it, the new belief will be lookin' CONVINCING. Which is what we want!

It Begins and Ends in the Subconscious Mind

One of my favorite quotes of all time is by Carl Jung: "The psychological rule says that when an inner situation is not made conscious, it happens outside, as fate. That is to say, when the individual remains undivided and does not become conscious of his inner opposite, the world must perforce act out the conflict and be torn into opposing halves."

Or, as this quote is commonly paraphrased: "Until you make the unconscious conscious, it will rule your life and you will call it fate."

Remember: Your subconscious is the storehouse of everything that's ever happened to you and around you, and as a result, it's a well-intentioned yet faulty command center, blocking and creating based on what feels safest. It loves patterns. It loves its beliefs. It loves to protect you based on memories.

Our subconscious minds have an astounding effect on our experienced reality—not just how we feel. One of my friends had a big career opportunity come up, one that would completely skyrocket her to a new dimension of her career dreams. All she needed to do was film a short video of herself sharing her story. Two minutes, maximum. She immediately found herself starting to panic about it, so she decided to practice and prep for it then devote the entire next day to filming.

Conveniently, when she woke up the next morning, she somehow had a mysterious allergic reaction on her face that rendered one-half of it puffy and red. Not really her lights-camera-action moment—there's no way she could film. She sent me a picture of her face, and I agreed she needed to see a doctor and get a prescription ASAP. We talked a little about how it was likely her subconscious because the timing was *too* uncanny and made plans to work on it with a tapping session when we saw each other later.

Later that day, I braced myself to see her, as she had told me several more times that the allergic reaction on her face had only gotten worse and worse. "It's SO bad," she told me over the phone, and I told her to just wear sunglasses. As I rounded the corner to greet her, I was immediately confused—her face looked completely fine. After a hug, I assessed. "Wait, *what's* the problem?" I asked, becoming Nancy Drew looking for clues and signs of this facial allergic reaction that knocked out her whole filming day.

"I know, I know. It's SO bad," she said, hiding her face. My jaw dropped. There was not a single sign of any allergic reaction. And yet, in the picture she took of her face, there had been significant swelling and redness. She was still seeing it, and I saw NOTHING.

So, what was true? Was her face really undergoing an allergic reaction? "Truth" doesn't matter so much here as experience: the allergic reaction popped up at exactly the right time to "protect" her from filming this reel that had the capacity to change her entire life.

One more example: a client of mine was hoping to sell her house and was feeling very frustrated that no offers were coming through. In a session, we explored how her subconscious could be creating a block, and realized it was a fear around a large lump sum of money coming in. We got to work clearing it, and toward the later part of the session, her phone rang loudly, interrupting us. She set it to the side to get to it later. Afterward, she texted me excitedly that the phone call had been from her real estate agent, sharing that she had received an offer on the house FAR above her asking price! Once her subconscious felt safe, the offer came through almost immediately.

Understanding your subconscious mind is like being given the keys to the castle where you can radically change your life. It makes *everything* make sense. As much as we think the subconscious is going rogue and wish it would just GET WITH THE PROGRAM so we can ascend to the life of our dreams—it's actually very, very intelligent. It's so good at protecting us . . . even when that protection is misguided and based on faulty information.

Just because it's faulty information doesn't mean your subconscious is doing anything wrong or bad. Imagine that a computer has a program on it that isn't working correctly. This would be because of the *coding* of that program. All it needs is a reprogramming. It will continue to run the faulty code time and time again until the code is rewritten—and this is no fault of the computer; it's just misinformation input by the engineer who entered the code. Once we understand where we got our own subconscious misinformation, and we trace it back to the root and clear it with our magic toolbox, the game really changes.

Too often we think that the roadblocks we stumble into must be fate. We start going after a dream career opportunity, only to experience disappointment and sticky energy. So we think it's "not meant to be."

We start dating yet another emotionally unavailable person who has an uncanny number of traits similar to the last individual who tore our hearts to smithereens. We think it's just how love is supposed to be for us.

We begin a new workout regimen or creative challenge, only to self-sabotage and give up within the first ten days, and think, "This is just who I am. I'm not a consistent person." Pulling us further into the story, into the identity, when actually, it's just a silly little cluster of beliefs, past experiences, and future expectations.

That cluster *can* be rewired and changed. *From the root.* To cause a shift in not just how you feel, but your entire experience of reality and everything you're calling in.

You're *never* stuck. You're *never* resigned to a fate you don't want. The Universe/God/Source/a Higher Power WANTS you to have everything you've ever wanted—because you are quite literally here for the expansion of consciousness. Your joy uplifts the world.

It's OLD, OUTDATED, and FALSE that things need to be difficult for you. It's time to start rethinking everything. What if the status quo hasn't been evidence of a disempowering story—just faulty lines of coding playing out? What if you can change all of it?

You can. You *are* the magic. So let's dive in.

CHAPTER REVIEW AND EXERCISES
TL;DR

• Our subconscious mind rules 95 percent of our reality. So, if we want to really change our lives, we have to look deeper. This is why solely conscious efforts to make big changes have their limits.

• The link between our subconscious mind and our life experience is undeniable. Life is reflecting our subconscious beliefs back to us all the time.

• Our subconscious minds are doing so much for us constantly. Yours never sleeps. It's taking care of keeping you alive and keeping you safe every moment of the day, without our conscious attention or acknowledgment.

• Our subconscious mind is a record of everything that has ever happened to us or has been observed around us. This influences our perception of the world. Everything that has happened has created our belief system.

• Beliefs begin at an early age and attract more and more evidence as self-fulfilling prophecies. Whatever we believe is true becomes true for us.

• This is why understanding and changing our subconscious beliefs is imperative for changing our lives.

Be[lie]f Detective Work

Choose TWO limiting beliefs you have about the world, yourself, and/or others. It could be anything. It could be the belief that it's hard to make money, that one-on-one friendships are better than friend groups, that monogamy isn't realistic . . . Any belief that isn't 100 percent serving you.

For the sake of it, play devil's advocate with yourself on this belief. Your subconscious is not used to this. It has, in fact, perfected the routine of confirming these belief systems. So throw it for a loop, for fun! Imagine that the belief has been proven to be a lie. What are other stories that could be plausible? Has there been any evidence to the contrary of this belief? Are you sure your sources here are sound?

Putting your belief on the "stand" and questioning it in your self-created "court of law" is a great way of proving to yourself that a belief is just something you've witnessed, that has been told to you, and/or that you have experienced a number of times. But just because you have evidence for it doesn't mean it has to be true. If the belief is not serving you, wouldn't you rather believe something else? Something more empowering? Give yourself the chance to view things differently. List out as many possible points of "counterevidence" or alternative stories as you can think of, and then let your mind continue to run in the background the rest of the day, thinking of more. If this is hard at first, GOOD! It's like you're stopping the gears that have been running in one direction in your brain for years to get them to go the other direction. This is where change begins.

PART 2

THE MAGIC TOOLBOX: REWIRE AND UPLEVEL

CHAPTER 4

THE SUBCONSCIOUS BREAKTHROUGH FORMULA

We all have clear turning points in our lives that create a marked difference. There was our life before a discovery or event . . . and then there was our life after. It was that significant. For me, my own axis-altering shift happened because of exactly what you're about to learn in this chapter. This information flipped my world on its head, helped me to understand why I was so stuck, and has become a foundational part of how I now show up to my life and make magic happen on an almost-daily basis. This is genuinely why I believe that we all have the power to change our lives, because it just makes so much sense.

It all started with one really bad year—truly, one of those times in your life when you end up in such a rut you don't know how you got there or how to get out. As I mentioned in chapter 1, my first dose of mindset magic my junior year of college opened new paths to me that I never could have seen coming, including a connection to an entrepreneurship community that was teeming with opportunity, like my first paid speaking engagement. I instantly fell in love with it, which led to yet another domino falling over. That community happened to be looking for a community manager, and in the summer before my senior year, I applied, flew to New York City for in-person interviews, and landed the role. To say this was a dream come true was an understatement. My role was to network and foster the sense of community, meaning I was always connecting with entrepreneurs and learning from them. It also happened to be an extremely lucrative part-time role, another wink that my mindset shift had worked (I'd also done an EFT Tapping session on money a few weeks before I got the job, which you'll learn all about soon).

I settled into my dream job, networking with amazing individuals doing truly extraordinary things. I'd take their calls walking from Italian class, sitting on the Main Green, or heading to the library to study. One interaction was with a book coach, who invited me to join his esteemed program, which would include me writing and developing a book to publish. Because everything was lining up so perfectly on this golden lifeline of serendipity, it made perfect sense to write a book about my research in college. I wrote my honors thesis and that book in parallel, on the topic of female self-agency in entrepreneurship and venture capital. Everything in my life blended together so cohesively that I couldn't have planned it better if I'd tried. I even rode that wave of ambition into creating an incubator on campus for female-identifying student entrepreneurs and applied those learnings to my research for the book and thesis as well. I go into great detail here to let you know: I was feeling pretty darn good about myself. I had a confidence about my future that felt supported left, right, up, and down, in every opportunity and connection in my life. My book was published just a few weeks after my college graduation, and I accepted a full-time role with the entrepreneurship community that started a few weeks after that. And then even more magic began to happen.

An entrepreneurship director at a college in Ohio read my book and messaged me asking for a phone call to see if I could come speak at his university. I hopped on the call excited to talk about the opportunity, thinking for sure it was unpaid but my travel would likely be covered. "How cool!" I thought to myself. "I get to travel and speak to students!" Toward the end of the call, he mentioned his budget, which, lo and behold, was nothing CLOSE to an unpaid speaking engagement in the best way possible. My jaw dropped. "Is that number okay?" he asked, as if he hadn't rocked my world by stating half of my monthly salary for just a few hours of my time doing what I genuinely love to do. Of course, I played it cool. "Sure, I can make that work," I said (suave) and saved my squealing for when I hung up the phone. This phone call also happened while I was sitting in my car in the parking lot of Einstein Bros. Bagels—and that's how I learned that the most life-changing opportunities can happen when you least expect it. It made for one celebratory bagel.

That was the first signal to me that I was onto something here. I began reaching out to colleges across the U.S., asking if I could come speak to their entrepreneurship students. I didn't ask for a penny at first; it was just my intention to get in front of students, hone my craft, and figure out what it means to be a speaker. Within weeks, I had a full-blown speaking tour booked across some epic colleges. The more I spoke, the more testimonials and footage I got, and my confidence rose enough for me to state my speaking fee—and many schools said yes! I became more excited about what I could do as a speaker and author with my personal brand, which led me to a crossroads: Do I continue in my full-time job or take the leap so I can really scale these big dreams? I asked for a unicorn as a sign I needed to quit, since I'd heard Gabby Bernstein, author of *The Universe Has Your Back*, say that she had asked for a sign of an owl if she should make a major decision. I was admittedly taunting the universe with the unicorn request, knowing I wasn't going to see one of those struttin' down the street. That night, I dreamt that there was a knock at my door. I opened it, and a unicorn was there; it then turned into an owl and flew into my face. Aggressive, but I got it. Could we be any more loud and clear?! (Maybe it was my subconscious, but that is fitting for this chapter.)

So I went for it. I quit my full-time job to bet on myself. It was one of the most terrifying decisions I'd ever made, but shortly after, I was rewarded for my bravery by landing a speaking gig for the same amount as my monthly salary. "Okay," I thought. "Maybe I can do this."

One problem: timing. I made this decision and transition in February, and colleges were finalizing their second semester programming . . . then wrapping up for the summer. Suddenly, what *had* been working beautifully and effortlessly was not working anymore. I wasn't going to be able to speak at any colleges for the summer or make a dime. I increasingly became more worried and desperate, sending out pitch emails like my life depended on it.

I had thought that all this extra time would be the world's most productive chapter of my life, but the compiling worry and stress was producing the opposite effect. I felt extremely heavy, all the time. I'd get bright ideas late at night for what I could do the next day to drive my career forward, conjuring an image of me waking up bright-eyed and bushy-tailed, making a big cup of coffee, and spending the day in a productive whir of new ideas, breakthroughs, and exciting "please come speak here!" emails. I'd then proceed to spend the whole next day feeling down and exhausted, no matter how much coffee I consumed. My motivation was zapped. Everything I did try to do felt like a dead end. It started to bring up some existential questions about what I really wanted to do with my life. Why was speaking so important to me? If I could wave a magic wand, what would I do for a living and LOVE? But the more the answers came to me, the more frightened and lost I felt. I knew it: I wanted to be an entertainer and a teacher. I wanted to be on camera. I wanted to move to a big city. These ambitions terrified me: they felt so beyond impossible that I was already experiencing disappointment even considering them.

After months of this, destiny intervened and I had my first EFT Tapping session with EFT practitioner Tiffany Jeffers. I had *no* idea on that first video call that she would become so important to me and completely change my life. At any time, any meeting or phone call or introduction (or book!) can turn our entire world around. I shared with her how I was feeling so stuck and down. And . . . we subconscious breakthrough'd it. We tapped through it. At this time, I was having physical symptoms from the emotional heaviness—I couldn't breathe out of my nose. I sounded like Rudolph the Red-Nosed Reindeer when I talked, and I looked puffy and swollen. Imagine having a sinus infection that just doesn't go away for months. After our first session, I could breathe out of my nose again! We did just a few sessions over the next few months, and in that time, what felt lost and hopeless suddenly began to turn a corner in an unexpected way. I reconnected spontaneously with an old writing connection, who asked if he could refer his clients to me for articles, and within a matter of weeks, I suddenly had dozens of clients and was making money again! This continued to unfold and accelerate, so much so that I began making my original salary—and then more and more. Schools started returning emails to book me for the fall semester. My "spark" returned. This opened the door for me to be able to move to New York City to really pursue my dreams—and afford that magical studio apartment. Within that year, my whole life changed. I started posting on social media and rapidly grew an audience. I started hitting record months in my income. I hit six figures in six months—when I'd been barely making a couple thousand a month from miscellaneous writing gigs during that deeply stuck phase. My entire face changed, and I began to look like a different person (turns out that being able to breathe through your nose can really help!). My new life in New York City commenced some of the happiest days of my life. I began feeling so much more peace and hope than I could have fathomed beforehand. I now live in my dream apartment in New York City, I have amazing best friends, I work on-camera for a living, and I run my dream business: a community called Dreamaway, where we do the exact process you're about to learn in this chapter on topics like love, worthiness, abundance, procrastination, self-concept, career, and so much more.

It all started with what you're about to learn—and every time I want to go deeper or aim higher, this is where I turn. It works that well. It leads to that many "aha" moments. I couldn't see it at the time, but looking back at this story through the lens of my subconscious breakthrough glasses, it's so obvious to me. I wasn't stuck because of timing. I was stuck because I was terrified. Once I quit my job, massive limiting beliefs came to the surface; I just didn't sit with myself long enough to realize I was battling with them. Deep down, I was terrified I'd made the wrong choice. I was terrified I couldn't be successful on my own. I was terrified the "luck" was going to run out. I thought that the terror came from the external series of events and the crickets in my inbox, but it was actually a *reflection* of my beliefs and fears. That's what caused such a marked shift. Timing wasn't out to get to me—my subconscious was running the show. This will become extremely obvious to you, too, as you read this next chapter, and I hope it excites you. When we realize why we're stuck, we suddenly have the keys to get unstuck. It's a fascinating journey within.

What if you already have the answers you seek within you? What if YOU have had the magic all along? That's what we're diving into: the breakthrough that's been waiting to happen.

The Subconscious Breakthrough Formula is built upon the premise that when we ask the subconscious a question, it always answers—even if it defeats itself in the process. Imagine you're pulling a heist (not that I think you'd do that, but bear with me here), and you're trying to find the key to a treasure chest. All you need is the key, and many jewels and diamonds await you. And then you notice: the key is in the hand of the treasure chest security guard. Under typical conditions, no one would go up to the security guard and say, "Hey, can I borrow that key?" unless they were really just goin' for it with no concern for the outcome. In which case, WOW, that's Audacity with a capital *A* and I respect it.

The subconscious is different. With the subconscious mind, WE are the master. WE hold the key. We can absolutely ask the inner security guard to give us the key and please unlock the treasure chest. And it'll say, "No problem, happy to do it!" and unlock it on the spot.

It *does* matter what questions you ask, and how you ask them. The Subconscious Breakthrough Formula tricks your subconscious into telling you exactly why it is the way it is—so that we can get in there and rewrite that faulty coding. Although the subconscious is quite literally underneath the conscious mind and therefore usually hiding from you, it still possesses the answers that you're looking for, and we can bring them up to the conscious mind at any time.

And honestly, the fact that the subconscious is underneath the surface is exactly what makes this work so interesting. I've been giving myself and clients subconscious breakthroughs for several years now, and it never fails to leave everyone "ooh-ing" and "ahh-ing." There is such a liberation that comes from identifying the block, memory, or limiting belief that's been causing a problem the entire time. The breakthrough is so inherently satisfying and comes with the promise of a new beginning.

So let's venture into your first breakthrough. All you need is a pen, a notebook, and a moment for just you. Put away all distractions. We're going on a treasure hunt.

I want you to think about **what you want most in the world right now**, at this moment. Fun, right?

It could be a career goal, like a promotion or for your business to hit a certain benchmark. It could be a relationship goal, like meeting The One or finally moving to the next level with someone special. It could be something super magical, like being able to travel the world for a year or having your movie script spontaneously discovered and made into a real motion picture or hosting your first fashion show.

Choose anything you deeply want that feels blocked, challenging, or next-level. You'd know it was blocked if it feels like you just can't get there or obstacles keep arising when you feel you're getting close.

Anything that's in the distance that feels bigger than you. Just choose one thing for now; you can come back and repeat this process with any or all of them soon.

Once you identify it, write it down.

Now, let's "subconscious breakthrough" this bad boy. Yes, I did make that a verb.

For each of the following questions, notice what immediately comes to mind as you read them in respect to your goal, and then take off and start journaling.

I want you to journal on each of these questions for *at least one page*, because again, we move past the conscious buffer when we're forced to keep digging. And as you journal, practice incredible self-acceptance and self-compassion. The more curious we can be, the better—but also, the more *neutral* we can be, the better. Because your responses aren't "good" or "bad." This isn't a test you'll get graded on. No one else is reading this but you. This is just a deep dive for information: the swirl of thoughts, feelings, memories, and beliefs that are right there beneath the surface.

Also, writing down limiting beliefs or potentially negative thoughts is okay! We are doing it for the sake of detective work. We can't understand what is going on underneath the surface until we bring it into the light of day, and journaling is a great way to process and see it. We oftentimes just need to get our thoughts and initial reactions on paper to understand what they are and help us dig deeper.

If you have concerns that writing them down will make them more real, you can always honor that belief by safely burning the paper afterward, or running water from the faucet over it, watching the ink melt and the paper disintegrate. But I assure you: journaling is a critical part of this process, and bringing a limiting belief to the conscious mind is no different from taking an X-ray at the doctor's office to see if a bone is broken. It's there either way, but when we can see it, we can do something about it.

Also, know that in the journaling process, you are already causing shifts. In the process of writing, our pen moves from the left to the right of the page, then again as we move down a line. And as we write, our eyes follow our pen. This movement of our eyes from left to right is a form of "bilateral stimulation," which is highly helpful for processing information because it engages the rational and logistical left side of the brain as well as our more creative and emotional side of the brain. You know how people say to "sleep on it" in regard to a big decision? This is because your REM (rapid eye movement) sleep helps your brain process information. While your eyes are closed, they're darting back and forth from the left to the right. Anything that involves both sides of our brain via bilateral stimulation (which, by the way, even includes walking or swimming!) helps us to process information and emotions.

You'll find more clarity as you continue to journal, and bringing these deeply buried subconscious beliefs to the surface also means you're bringing them to your prefrontal cortex. When you can consciously assess what the belief is, it's possible your reaction could be something like, "WHAT? This silly belief has been in there all along?" Or maybe it will hit you like a steamroller and come packed with emotions. Honor it all. The new awareness is a shift within itself.

As you'll learn more about soon, your beliefs are held in place by strong emotions, which is why Emotional Freedom Technique (EFT) Tapping is the bedrock methodology of this process, this book, my life, and rewiring. (Casual.) Be kind to yourself as these emotions emerge, and please, keep it light as you begin this process for the first time. If something becomes very emotional for you, try turning on some happy music, going for a walk outside, taking a cold shower, coloring or drawing, or getting a cuddle from a pet or a stuffed animal. As always, please prioritize your own well-being and as mentioned in the Author's Note on Safety at the beginning of the book, seek a licensed therapist for this work if you suspect traumatic memories may be beneath the surface.

Now, let's descend into the subconscious . . .

Your Subconscious Breakthrough Questions

Question 1. What bad thing happens if this goal comes to fruition? Yes, I said BAD THING! What could potentially go wrong?

Question 2. What do you believe you need to GIVE UP that you currently LIKE about your life in order to bring this in?

Question 3. WHY does it make sense mentally that this is blocked for you? What is the evidence that you have for why this should be difficult or impossible? (This could be what someone has said to you in the past, your lack of positive examples of people who have done it, or any other beliefs.)

Question 4. What is an example of a time in the past when you also felt this way? (It could be related or absolutely wildly unrelated.)

Question 5. How would a new belief—or getting what you REALLY want—be a mismatch for your identity and self-concept?

UNDERSTANDING THE QUESTIONS
AND YOUR ANSWERS

Each of these questions has been perfectly worded to help us to unearth your subconscious motivations. Remember: Your subconscious mind has *one* main prerogative. That is, above all, to keep you alive. In order to do so, it *must* keep you safe. It will put safety above happiness every single time . . . which means, to put it another way, that your subconscious actually doesn't care at all about your happiness or self-actualization or your big dreams. Really, it would prefer you stay at home safe and cozy and do nothing big or exciting or expansive with your life. Because that's what will have the *highest chance* of keeping you safe.

To the subconscious, "safe" doesn't just mean staying in bed, cozy with the doors locked, away from any potential physical dangers. It also means emotionally safe. The subconscious deems rejection as dangerous because we are biologically programmed to seek acceptance and community. Anything that your subconscious feels could threaten that acceptance—such as a big rejection, people judging us, or the possibility of a romantic partner shattering our hearts—sends the subconscious into alarm mode. This is also why a common feeling associated with major heartbreak is anxiety.

But each of our individual subconscious minds responds differently. None of this is one size fits all. That's why you have a friend who is so "lucky in love" and another friend who easily achieves career wins. It's just a reflection of their subconscious beliefs, and how their subconscious minds react to stimuli, such as a partner or a career opportunity.

The two consistencies among all subconscious minds:

1. They want to keep us safe, and
2. They do so according to the bank of information they have from past experiences.

What we have lived, seen, observed, heard, and experienced creates our subconscious beliefs. While there are archetypal subconscious beliefs that many of us share and will have in common, the truth is we also all have differing subconscious beliefs. Our reasons and evidence for these beliefs are always dependent on *personal experience*. This is what makes the Subconscious Breakthrough Formula so important: we're understanding how our own conceptions of the world and previous experiences have shaped our beliefs and, therefore, what we can call in or attain.

What we believe is ALWAYS what we will experience. Even if the belief isn't "true." Look at the word *believe*, or *belief*—there's a "lie" in the middle. It's up to us to learn to understand which beliefs aren't serving us and how to rewire them from the root so our beliefs become more empowering and get us to where we want to go.

Question I. What bad thing happens if this goal comes to fruition?

This is the most common question I use in subconscious breakthroughs. It seems backwards, I know. How could this big sparkly magical wish I've always wanted potentially have a downside? On first conscious glance, goals like wanting more money or marrying your soulmate seem all good, with no potential downside.

But if these goals are continuously blocked, it is more than likely because your subconscious believes "bad things" will happen if you attain them.

When a desire, dream, or goal is blocked and perpetually unfulfilled, it's because the conscious and the subconscious are at odds. Your subconscious mind wants something different from what your conscious mind wants.

As an example of this, one of my best friends has struggled for a long time with wanting to make more money. In fact, she NEEDED to make more because she was swimming in debt from student loans and credit cards. But time and time again, she was dealt a bad financial hand. Promised raises at her job didn't come through. Freelance work proved hard to find, and when she did find it, the money was scant. Luckily, her best friend is a subconscious breakthrough coach (hi, it's me), so one morning in my apartment, we made some frothy cups of coffee and I got to my detective work.

It didn't make sense. Why wouldn't her subconscious want more money? More money *should* equate with more financial security. She needed to pay off large debts and loans. She was working so hard, at her nine-to-five *and* with side hustles . . . and yet, nothing. Nothing moved the needle forward.

She had even moved cities to downsize her apartment, which cut her monthly rent in half, but despite what should have been a financial leg up, she was *still* coming up short every single month and falling deeper into debt. It was as if she never moved and halved that monthly expense at all. She just kept getting the same financial outcome, and she was so deeply frustrated. I watched her eyes fill to the brim with tears as we started talking about the fear, frustration, and deep sadness.

And then, as it always does, a light-bulb moment occurred thanks to the Subconscious Breakthrough Formula. As we explored what bad things could happen if her money soared, family relationships came to the forefront. Specifically, her relationship with her mom. She began recounting many common statements her mom would repeat over the course of her entire life about wealthy people. They had grown up struggling, and her mother's perception of those who do make plenty of money was . . . less than pleasant.

Her subconscious mind had taken in this information and formed a belief: "If I begin to make more money, I will become the type of person my mother speaks poorly about." What logically followed from this was "My mother will no longer love and accept me."

This was deep. It all began to make so much sense. No wonder her subconscious was getting rid of money as quickly as it came in and blocking every potential chance to make more. It was trying to keep her *safe*. And this safety was tied to a parent—which is a very, very primal need. For the first part of our lives, we are wholly dependent on our parents or primary caregivers for everything. At four years old we can't say, "Screw it, see y'all later" and walk out of the house to fend for ourselves. When we are dependent on someone, we KNOW our survival is linked to them providing for us. They're also our first foray into the world at large, and as children, we don't have critical thinking skills. If a parent says, "Wealthy people suck," we take that on as truth. We don't start critically thinking it through, like, "Hold on a second, didn't we recently hear of someone we respect having a financial windfall and dedicating some of it to a great cause?" or, "Wait, my friend at school comes from a wealthy family, and every time I go over to their house for a playdate, they're all so nice to me."

Multiple truths can exist at once, and we usually do have differing pieces of evidence. We have what we hear from our parents/caregivers, then our own experiences. But our experiences are highly likely to mirror our beliefs, because our reticular activating systems are looking for evidence on what's already in there. This is why our parents or early caretakers are so influential on our life experience—they create the foundational bedrock of our perception of the world with their own beliefs and comments, which we take on as truth. Even just the *perception* that our parents or early caretakers believe something can begin a neural pathway of a belief at a young age that shapes our entire lives until we identify and rewire it.

In the case of my best friend, she had multiple beliefs and thoughts about making more money. She wanted it. She had many friends who were wealthy. She didn't necessarily share the same views of wealthy people as her mother. But she knew her mom believed it, and therefore, her subconscious mind had equated keeping her mother's love and acceptance with staying broke and in debt.

As I will continue to say many times: just because we believe something DOES NOT mean it's true. There is a possible world in which she can absolutely make more money and actually have an *improved* relationship with her mother as a result, even though that felt less than likely in the moment. But there are always possibilities. Nothing is impossible, especially in this work.

So, we began to rewire this belief and fear and did some EFT Tapping on it (as you'll learn in the next chapter!). And afterward, things rapidly began to shift. She was originally making $30 per freelance article, and within the next few months, she landed a gig for $300 per freelance article. Ten times the income! She was offered a new job at a higher salary and recently got a large end-of-the-year bonus and another raise. What used to feel so blocked and impossible is now easy and natural for her and growing every single day, especially as she continues this work. And, through it all, her relationship with her mom stays strong. She has not lost even a fraction of her mom's love and acceptance, and she's showing her mom what's possible.

She needed to understand what her subconscious believed would happen in order to clear it from the root, and this magical question "What bad thing happens?" led to a powerful breakthrough, release, rewire, and a shift into an entirely new reality with more empowering experiences.

Question 2. What do you believe you need to GIVE UP that you currently LIKE about your life in order to bring this in?

The writer Brianna Wiest once said, "Your new life is going to cost you your old one." A lot of times, this quote might feel like a no-brainer. You might say, "Sure—you can take this 'old life'! I DON'T WANT IT!"

To our conscious mind, that's like someone saying, "Sure, you can get this gorgeous, shiny pair of red stilettos you've always wanted, but it's going to cost you your ratty old slippers that are covered in cat hair." What's the catch?!

Well . . . your subconscious mind isn't always on board with this trade-off. Because that old life is actually super familiar, comfortable, and predictable. Just like that old ratty pair of slippers. Which would you rather wear standing for eight hours—brand-new stilettos or broken-in slippers? It's like that to the subconscious. It's all about comfort.

Here are some examples of how the subconscious mind may perceive what's being given up. I will be playing the role of your subconscious mind. Feel free to give it a fun dramatic timbre as you read it in your head.

For calling in your soulmate . . .

- "Oh no, so much for those solo nights I loved so much. Now I'm always going to have someone in my space."

- "Well, I might as well give up on my goals if I call this in! I always focus better when I'm single and I'm not distracted with a partner."

- "I'd rather just be alone than always be worrying about my partner and what they're doing. I'll be giving up the peace of not having to wonder if my partner is talking to someone else or liking some rando's Instagram pics."

- "Ugh, I do not want to have to sacrifice my peace to tend to someone else's emotional needs."

- "Relationships are so much drama! Single life feels like smooth sailing right now."

- "Dating is FUN! My whole roster will go down the drain if I meet The One, and then I'll have to commit—I don't think I'm ready to give up that freedom!"

- "Even though I really want to meet my soulmate, I'm terrified they'll hurt me, or change their mind, or do one of the million things my ex did. It's really just safer to . . . not."

For manifesting a career uplevel . . .

- "This new level is going to require so much more responsibility. It feels easier and safer to just stay here and keep my current work-life balance."

• "So much more will be expected of me at this next level! I don't want to give up feeling like a big fish in a small pond. It's too much pressure."

• "This new role requires a lot more visibility, and that feels terrifying. Even though I'm not totally fulfilled with where I am now, at least I have fewer eyes on me."

• "What if I can't do it and perform at this next level? It feels easier to stay here and always be wondering what could be rather than actually going for it and falling flat on my face."

• "None of my friends have a job at that level. This will separate me from them, and they might be jealous, or we might not be able to relate to each other anymore."

• "I'm not sure this is the field I want to stay in forever. . . . It may be harder to leave this industry if I get this promotion."

• "What if I uplevel and hate it and I can't get back to where I am now? I kinda like where I am now . . ."

For calling in more money . . .

• "I've only ever seen people make more money by working harder. I really don't want to have to work harder!"

• "More money = more problems. Not sure what those problems are, but they sound bad, and I'd rather not have any problems."

• "If I start making more money, I'll need to figure out how to manage my money and invest. That sounds way too difficult."

• "The more money I make, the more I'll have to pay in taxes, and that freaks me out!"

• "If I start making more money, my friends and family won't be able to relate to me, and they'll become jealous. It will force me to give up the peace and common life experience I have with them."

• "If I make more money, everyone will expect me to pay for everything, and that is so much responsibility. I don't want to give up how things are right now."

Now you see why your subconscious is afraid. For every single thing you want, there's something you're also giving up. But this is OKAY. It's natural. Life should always be a beautiful recycling process. Even as you've been reading this chapter, you've been recycling by breathing in new oxygen and breathing out carbon dioxide. You are used to the release of the old and outdated for the new.

Question 3. WHY does it make sense mentally that this is blocked for you? What is the evidence that you have for why this should be difficult or impossible?

Remember, your subconscious has been compiling data and information your entire life that has constructed your worldview. And so much of this has come from other people. We witness how others interact with the world from a young age—we see what they believe is possible, what they say, how they act—and that becomes our barometer for how we should view ourselves in the world.

So many of our early experiences have come together to create this. One story that comes to mind is from a Dreamaway member, Jenn. Jenn was hoping to bring more abundance into her life, but she was struggling with it and felt a lot of shame attached. And as she dug deeper into her subconscious beliefs during my "Slingshot Sleepover" program, it made sense:

"As I did your program, a limiting belief around the fear of success kept coming up," she shared with me. "I didn't understand that at all but worked on it and realized it was tied to watching my parents go bankrupt as a kid. I was afraid to have anything great financially because I was so scared it would all be taken away or that I could lose it one day. And I realized I had been keeping myself 'safe' living paycheck to paycheck."

Her subconscious had taken on the experience of witnessing her parents go bankrupt and had interpreted, through its limited lens, that large sums of money were dangerous. The belief: "I can't handle a great amount of money, because I'll lose it."

Does it make logical sense that making *less* money could keep us financially *more* safe? Not really. But the subconscious mind doesn't care about logic. "I saw what I saw and that means what I think it means!" it says, like a toddler crossing its arms and pouting. (It reasons like a toddler, too. No offense, Subconscious.)

Once Jenn was able to pinpoint what the belief was and where it came from, she was able to clear it using EFT Tapping. (We're so close to learning how to do this, don't worry!)

Within two weeks of completing the tapping program, her boss spontaneously awarded her an off-cycle bonus of $17,000. Which was not normal or expected.

"I was so stunned!" she told me. I would be, too!

The Subconscious Breakthrough Formula had worked yet again: something was difficult (finances—expressed as living paycheck to paycheck, with only just enough to get by and never more).

Deeper analysis revealed that the opposite had been modeled to her and had been marked in red ink in her subconscious mind as *dangerous*.

Therefore, her subconscious had come up with an easy way to stay safe: avoid great sums of money.

This could only be changed by changing her *subconscious perception* of money.

Where Was the Difficulty Modeled?

There is no limit to the reasons your goal or dream might seem impossible or difficult to you: family, your immediate friend group, and your own experiences.

A school counselor who laughed in your face when you said which college you wanted to go to. Internalization: I'll never be enough to get to where I want to go.

A verbally abrasive sports coach who always made you feel like you were falling behind. Internalization: I can't keep up, and I'm scared to be watched as I'm trying.

Your parents getting divorced, leaving one parent heartbroken and never opening their heart again. Internalization: Love is dangerous. I'm one heartbreak away from never being able to love again.

An entrepreneurial parent constantly complaining that sales are slow and it's impossible to "make it" unless you're in the top 1 percent. Internalization: I couldn't possibly be successful in business if my parent couldn't.

A play you auditioned for but lost the part to someone seemingly more talented, more beautiful, more graceful, you name it. Internalization: Someone out there who is "better" than me wants what I want, too, and is going to get it over me.

You likely have MANY, MANY past experiences of getting blocked or witnessing difficulty and hardship in exactly what it is you're trying to bring to fruition.

These could be experiences that date back as far as elementary school or early childhood. I hear all the time when working with clients things like, "Well, this kind of reminds me of when I was so excited about my project for the science fair in third grade and worked on it nonstop for two weeks, only to not win, which was really crushing at the time. But that was third grade! That doesn't matter."

Actually, yes, it does matter. It matters very much. In said example, the subconscious mind internalized something BIG: "It doesn't matter how hard I work. I'm not a winner. I can't achieve what I want."

This belief can manifest itself in all types of behaviors: "laziness," procrastination, never going after the dream or goal. OR continuing along in the same hustle mentality, working REALLY hard, but always having the same outcome occur: a disappointing one.

The truth is, just because it's BEEN blocked doesn't mean it has to continue to be blocked. We do not have to honor our past stories—or the stories of others—by repeating them in order to "stay safe." It's plenty safe to choose a new story and a new experience, despite the past.

But the subconscious gets stuck in its circles, around and around on a racetrack, repeating what has happened or what it's seen. Because as long as it's lived it or seen others live it, even if it was a capital-M *Miserable* experience, it is verified as "safe."

In other words: it never wants you to get anywhere *near* a potential spouse, an audition opportunity, a promotion, or a business idea because of the danger it believes it has witnessed or experienced, or simply the danger of the unknown.

Which leads us to the next question:

Question 4. What is an example of a time in the past when you also felt this way?

Remember: your subconscious mind is operating on what it already contains within it, like a line of computer code. It continues to run the same code over and over again, even if it is faulty code that isn't producing the results you want. Just like a computer doesn't know that a bad line of code is faulty, your subconscious mind doesn't know that the old stories you've been living by aren't ideal. Even if you keep getting what you don't want out of them.

This is why it's so important to find the root—figure out when the code was entered. In other words, before I go too wild with this metaphor, to figure out when you learned, internalized, or perceived the belief your subconscious is now operating by. For example, imagine that Maria keeps getting passed up for a promotion at her law firm. Every time she thinks she's about to make partner, they promote someone else instead. This makes her feel "second best," "overlooked," and "never quite good enough."

If I was walking Maria through a subconscious breakthrough, I'd ask her—when is a time in the past you felt second best, overlooked, and never quite good enough? She could then follow this emotion back to a totally different experience in a totally different phase of her life. Perhaps she felt the same way in law school, and another student always seemed to be the professor's favorite no matter how hard Maria worked. Now, her subconscious is recreating this experience again in a brand-new environment, with all new people—because it's the "line of code" her subconscious is living by.

However, as a very thorough coach, I wouldn't be satisfied just going back to law school. Because we are in a theta brainwave state up until age seven, our subconscious minds are WIDE open to suggestion during this time, which means they take on all types of faulty code in these critical years. Now, in your adult years, your brain has a Critical Faculty that makes it less likely to take on a statement as truth without questioning it. Think of the Critical Faculty as a gatekeeper who won't take on information unless it's aligned with evidence you already have and is logically sound. If someone came up to you right now and said, "Dragons are real and I have one as a pet," you wouldn't believe them because you already have plenty of evidence that dragons are not, in fact, real. (Do we *really* know, though? But that's a different discussion!) Your Critical Faculty would block this information with its existing knowledge.

But if you were five years old and someone with authority—like a parent or a teacher—told you that dragons were real, you would absolutely believe them. Your Critical Faculty hasn't been trained yet, and so your brain would be less likely to question them, because you're wide open to new information without many references yet that you can use to judge and assess the information coming in through a critical lens.

The issue here is that during this critical time up to age seven, we tend to take on beliefs that are absolutely *not true* and are inherently limited and limiting. Our subconscious perceives early experiences without the Critical Faculty to say "Hmm, is this REALLY true?" And this is how the early lines of code are written in our brains.

So, going back to the example of Maria, I'd want to know what very early life experiences she had where she felt second best, overlooked, and never quite good enough. And, *oh!* Lo and behold—imagine Maria has a sibling who was a child prodigy and could tickle the piano keys like nobody's business. And Maria's parents, who were also very artistic and into music, gave this sibling a great deal of attention, affection, and praise as a result. So Maria constantly felt second best, overlooked, and never quite good enough. How could her dazzling good grades in school compare to her sibling being the next Mozart?

Now, is this the *truth*? Is Maria really second best, overlooked, and never quite good enough? Absolutely not. But it makes sense how she could perceive that if there was an unequal allocation of attention onto her sibling. If you asked her parents, they'd likely say they didn't mean for it to be perceived this way at all and they were just trying to support her sibling's dream through the many piano recitals and music-related opportunities while Maria seemed very self-sufficient and involved with her studies.

Unconsciously, though, this line of code has continuously played out over Maria's life. She has continued to attract similar situations to this initial experience—not because it's true that she is second best, but because it's what her subconscious has internalized from these early childhood experiences. The logic of it makes sense, even if it isn't true.

Until we are able to identify the cause of a subconscious belief and pattern and then clear it from the root, we'll keep encountering it over and over again. It's like trying to print out a piece of paper from your computer and getting frustrated that there's a typo in one of the words. Continuing to print out more and more copies isn't going to fix the typo—but going back into your document, finding the word, and correcting the error will.

In life, the printer continuing to print out the typo again and again can show up in our experiences in multiple ways. For example, maybe Maria started to experience feeling second best during Debate Club in middle school, following these early childhood experiences with her sibling. Then, perhaps she met someone she really liked romantically, but it quickly ended because her partner wasn't over their ex. She perceived this as another example of being second best. Then, of course, it's started showing up once again in her profession, as she keeps getting passed over for the promotion she wants.

Now, her brain has an exhaustive list of compelling evidence as to why she is second best. The initial experience with her sibling created the neural pathway, and everything that happened after that strengthened the neural pathway. And while it was never actually true, her subconscious doesn't care! If it's in the program, it will keep coming out every time.

As you begin to uncover your own patterns and "typos" in the system, it's important to note that your subconscious mind also can't fully tell the difference between multiple areas of your life. It doesn't have one walled-off section for your love life and another for your career. It all blends together. Because of this, a way you felt in one area of your life may be repeated in another. In the example of Maria, feeling second best had reverberations across her family life, love life, and career. One of my clients experienced exactly this following a heartbreak. She was looking for a job and it was causing her a great deal of anxiety because she believed that her lack of experience in her field would be a detrimental factor in her applications. She didn't feel worthy of landing a job in her field. One day, we had a quick EFT Tapping session together and cleared many of these feelings. Later that afternoon, she received a job offer!

However, her new job didn't completely alleviate the feeling of unworthiness. Although the subconscious shift had finally landed her a job, she really desired a higher salary. As she dove deeper into her subconscious, she found something fascinating: the feeling of unworthiness related to her salary actually echoed her first major heartbreak. "I'd felt a lot of anxiety in the relationship, and then ultimately, I felt burned and abandoned in the breakup," she explained to me. "I was experiencing the same in my career—first with landing a job, and then with trying to get a higher salary."

Because blocks are seldom just about one area of our lives, she was able to connect that feeling of unworthiness from her heartbreak to how she was feeling in all her relationships, across her friends and her family. In all these interpersonal dynamics, her brain had equated her low salary as a reflection of her worth—and her subconscious had the evidence for it. So, she went within to heal her feeling of worthiness. She focused her attention on healing and releasing the core feelings that the heartbreak had stirred within her, how they connected to her friendships and family dynamics, and within a month, she landed a job with a 50 percent increase from her original salary.

So, with the current block you are experiencing, try on your exploratory, investigative hat. Let the feeling and emotion bring valuable information to the surface.

Here are some questions you can ask yourself:

1. **If this feeling could speak, what would it say?** As you lean into the feeling, search for any extra information. A few fragmented words and phrases may come to the surface. It may make complete sense, or it may make barely any sense. Just see if anything is connected. Examples here could include "I don't feel important," or "Be careful."

2. **How would I explain this situation and the way it makes me feel to a small child?** This approach is so potent for zeroing in on a key feeling. The subconscious mind can be quite basic, in somewhat of a childlike state. Because of this, it communicates mainly in symbols and metaphors. If you were to explain an emotionally challenging situation in your adult relationship to a five-year-old, you probably wouldn't say, "It makes me feel like the previous confines of our relationship are no longer applicable, even though we worked so diligently to create an open space for communication and support. But this recent betrayal has changed this dynamic." The five-year-old would look at you like you just grew a unicorn horn. Other adults only understand you because you're discussing it in very intellectual terms.

   However, you *could* say to a small child, "It makes me feel like I can't play with my best friend on the playground anymore." That one packs a punch. It's a metaphor, but it's a universal feeling.

   This question helps you get to the heart of the matter. Your answer doesn't have to be strictly in childlike terms, like referring to playgrounds or stuffed animals or summer break. But the simpler and closer to the heart it can be, the better. Such as "It makes me feel like I'm in my room alone and no one is coming to check on me," or, very simply, "It makes me feel sad."

3. **If this feeling was a copy-paste of a past feeling from a previous situation, what would it be? What does this entire situation remind me of?** Answering the first two questions can really help bring this third question home. The more we can get to the heart of a feeling, the more we can see how this feeling has been a thread woven through multiple experiences. The emotion itself holds so much information in its DNA. As you lean into the feeling, explore whether it reminds you of anything else. Once again, it could be directly related to the unique "brand" of situation (e.g., career or relationship related), or it could be completely different.

This is also a profound way to find related memories that could be contributing to the fear or limiting belief. For example, as I've been pursuing my music dreams, it's been fascinating to notice when I recoil away from taking brave action or putting myself out there as a musician. Upon further investigation, I realized the feeling felt like a feeling I had when I was about four years old.

I was taking a violin class and I absolutely hated the violin. I didn't feel like I had a knack for it at all—it sounded like a squeaky hamster heaving in a cardio class when I would try to play. So, as you can imagine, I felt terrified for the big recital day, when all the parents would come in and hear what we had learned. Over two decades later, the memory of the nerves I felt the night before the performance and the feeling of absolutely not wanting to do something was showing up in something only slightly adjacent: a totally different kind of music. Except this time, I *did* want to sing in front of others and share my songs. But my subconscious searched through its filing system of related experiences—performing music—and triggered a deep feeling that I was about to do something I didn't want to do and that (I perceived) I wasn't particularly talented with. Going back and healing this core memory did wonders! All it took was cleaning up the faulty coding and assuring my subconscious I never have to pick up a violin again.

Question 5. How would a new belief—or getting what you REALLY want—be a mismatch for your identity and self-concept?

Finally, identity cannot be understated in all of this. One of the most common phrases I hear from those doing this rewiring work is "I'm having a really hard time envisioning that this could actually happen for me." They'll visualize it, but there's an inherent mismatch where it just seems too far out of the realm of what could happen, or they have a hard time embodying what they can conjure in their mind's eye. I've experienced this many times—and continue to!

This is because we form our self-concept based on everything that's ever happened—or not happened—for us. Even if it had NOTHING to do with us and our worth, our brains have been taking in the information through the lens of "What does this mean about me?"

I was recently talking with a friend who shared that she has a hard time believing she is worthy of luxury experiences because when she was growing up, her parents would always go with the cheapest possible option for everything: hotels, restaurants, clothes, you name it. Now, as an adult, she's struggling with feeling confident in raising her money ceiling or purchasing luxury items for herself. As a child, she internalized that her parents' spending choices were about what *she* was worth, when really, it was about their own money mindset.

This needs to be rewired in order for her to call in a new experience and feel comfortable with luxury. We all have stories that are similar to this in money and in other areas of life.

Similarly, one of my clients, Camille, was struggling after three years of casting calls for her dreams of being a model and nothing to show for it. With each rejection, she believed she was compiling more and more evidence for the core belief that she was not good enough. She took this on as an identity, believing she wasn't the "chosen one." The more she internalized this from the lack of results, the more it spiraled. Suddenly, she created a perception of models who book gigs as "celebrities," which placed her dream on an even higher pedestal. She was signed to a small modeling agency but was only booking free photoshoots. This also started to create the belief that she wasn't worthy of getting paid for her modeling work.

Once she identified these gaps in her identity, she pinpointed the limiting beliefs associated—the "reasoning," so to speak, why she might be experiencing all these challenges with her dream career. As a child, she had modeled for several different brands, but she began to lose her confidence as a teenager when the rejections first started. This took on a snowball effect; the more her confidence was shaken, the more she got rejected.

As she found and cleared the core beliefs—which took her several months of consistent investigative work and EFT Tapping—she finally got the call she had been waiting for. Her agency called her and shared that a major client booked her for a modeling gig—for a *big* campaign. So big that her photo ended up on billboards and every bus stop in her country of France!

Now, she lives in Paris and her modeling career is thriving. She even got to appear on TV for another campaign and is signed with multiple big-deal modeling agencies!

Camille's story illustrates the power and importance of taking a quick pause when things aren't going well to identify any existing identity blocks that are getting in the way. In her case, her blocks originated in her teenage years and had been just underneath the surface, blocking any potential new opportunity. It just took some subconscious mind "tune-ups" to bring her into alignment with her desired identity, and within months, that manifested in her reality, as well.

You can identify your perceived identity and self-concept by making the following statement for each major "bucket" of your life:

In (this area of life), I'm the type of person who . . .

Free write at least eight answers to this, filling in the blank. Again, we want to dig deeper, and pushing ourselves to keep journaling on this even when we don't know what else to write down is a great way to uncover something that's hiding just beneath the surface.

Try it for the following areas of life . . .

> In love, I'm the type of person who . . .
>
> In my career, I'm the type of person who . . .
>
> In my family, I'm the type of person who . . .
>
> In health, I'm the type of person who . . .
>
> In creativity, I'm the type of person who . . .
>
> In finances, I'm the type of person who . . .
>
> In friendships, I'm the type of person who . . .
>
> In habits, I'm the type of person who . . .
>
> In big-dream pursuits, I'm the type of person who . . .

Zero in on the topics that feel most important to you right now. For everything you write down, put on your Detective Hat again to seek the evidence. You didn't get this concept from nowhere! Tracing it back to where it originated is key in understanding the shaping of your subconscious mind.

I like to lovingly refer to all your answers to the collective subconscious breakthrough question as a "No wonder!" In other words, NO WONDER this has been so blocked! Really, try exclaiming that out loud for everything you've uncovered. It injects a lightness into the breakthrough. I think there's nothing quite as exciting as peeling back these "No wonder!"s because, as you're about to (finally!) learn, now all you have to do is release it and write a brand-new story.

CHAPTER REVIEW AND EXERCISES
TL;DR

• When we ask our subconscious mind a question, it always answers—which we can use to our advantage to uncover the sneaky, unconscious reasons why something has been blocked in our lives, or why the same pattern continues to repeat itself.

• Our subconscious is always trying to keep us safe, which means it values the familiar and predictable over the new, as exciting as the new can be. We can have compassion for this and allow it to guide our discovery process.

• Everything we want also has a potential downside to our subconscious mind. It's important to understand what those fears are and where they stem from so that we can clear them.

• Past experiences can repeat themselves in different "fonts" throughout our lives, so it's important to follow the core feeling or metaphor to understand where it originated.

• Awareness is the shift. Having these "No wonder!" moments will make everything click for you. From there, we can utilize EFT Tapping to rewire.

This Ain't Your First Rodeo

For this exercise, you're going to be understanding how you're living on "repeat" from an earlier experience. Begin by choosing a situation in your life that is causing you trouble. This could be a feeling of stagnancy with your career, an ongoing disagreement with a partner, or another unexpected expense just when your finances felt like they were getting back on track.

Let's get to the heart of it. How would you describe this situation to a small child? How does it feel to you? Metaphors here are important.

An example: Someone felt like their finances were finally turning around and their savings account was getting back into a good place. Then, their car broke down and the repairs set them back to exactly where they were before.

They do this exercise, and it yields the following:

"It feels like when I was a kid and I went to check my piggy bank, thinking it was totally full of quarters and other coins, but my brother had taken them and I was horrified to find it empty."

The core feeling: "I feel powerless in money, like others can take from me when I feel secure."

DING DING DING! The feeling can be traced back.

The next chapter on EFT Tapping will be so powerful to clear this memory from the root. But in the meantime, any memory you find from the past can be tended to with care and love via reimagining. Because you've become astute with visualizing the future, we can apply the same practices to revisualize the past.

Go back in time and imagine that the situation happened in an entirely different way. For the piggy bank example, maybe it could be reimagined that the individual's brother had actually taken the quarters to a coin machine to get her cash so she could more easily transport the money to the toy store, so the reason the piggy bank felt so light was because it was filled with dollars, not clanky, heavy coins.

It could be anything! This is a technique commonly used in hypnosis. When we reimagine the past, it actually does change our neural pathways. You're more likely to remember it differently the next time it comes to mind. Active rewiring!

CHAPTER 5

THE TOOL THAT CHANGED MY LIFE: EFT TAPPING

I used to have paralyzing test anxiety. It started my freshman year of college. A big midterm date would loom ahead of me, making it difficult to breathe or think or do anything but fervently study in an attempt to feel in control. Of course, studying only does so much when one's nervous system is highly activated. When your brain thinks it's fending off a saber-toothed tiger, it turns out it doesn't do its best job of absorbing macroeconomics principles.

The mere *mention* of an upcoming test could cause the anxiety to snowball. "Just a few hours left!" my well-intentioned college boyfriend said to me at breakfast the morning of the dreaded exam. He was just stating a fact (we had the class together and were going to take the exam together), but I immediately felt the blood drain from my face as if I were about to jump out of an airplane and he had just said "just a few seconds left till we catapult toward the ground!" I proceeded to spend the next twenty minutes having an anxiety attack in the restaurant bathroom, trying to compose myself and get the tears under control.

It made no logical sense. It was just a test. I was incredible at studying. I took diligent notes every single lecture. I was quite literally an A+ student and a teacher's pet.

I get my academic prowess from my mom—she was a stellar student herself. And my mom is actually the reason this entire story turns around. She had stumbled across a methodology called EFT Tapping, which already had a growing body of supportive research into its efficacy for alleviating anxiety, depression, PTSD, and more. She figured it was worth a try for the test anxiety I was experiencing, and she signed me up for a session.

I had a last-minute EFT session with an EFT practitioner in the nick of time, just two hours before the exam. I'll never forget the panic that was flooding my whole body. But then, through just a few rounds of tapping, I calmed down until I was in a regulated state. I watched the minutes tick down to test time and got ready to meet my boyfriend, who was bracing himself to assist in my assured meltdown that was only seconds away from detonating, to walk to the classroom. But, to his shock and surprise, there was a complete shift in my emotions and even my body language from the Great Crying in the Restaurant Bathroom Scene mere hours earlier. "What just happened?!" he asked.

I whizzed through that exam with flying colors. I *aced* it. But what's more is I felt so calm, and almost gleeful, as I took it. I remember the awe as I scanned my body as we got into the classroom and took our seats. I was . . . fine. I couldn't summon the feeling of anxiety in my body even when I tried.

I scanned my body again as the professor handed out the exam. Nothing. Then again as we officially started taking the test. Nothing.

I knew every single answer, and my brain could calmly peruse its database built by my many hours of studying. I couldn't believe how easy it was, and my confidence grew by the second. A moment I was dreading, losing sleep over, and refusing a perfectly good waffle over, had actually become a satisfying, empowering moment of "Whoa! I got this." How is this even possible?

EFT Tapping

Meet the tool that changed my life entirely and will absolutely change yours. EFT Tapping, otherwise known as "Emotional Freedom Technique," is a methodology akin to "emotional acupuncture" and is rooted in traditional Chinese medicine. If you've ever had an acupuncture appointment, you know that the microneedles are placed in specific meridian points of the body. We have hundreds of these points, and they correspond with different organs, systems, and bodily processes.

Acupuncture works by stimulating the flow of energy between these meridian points. Think of each meridian point as an important juncture along the "energy highways" of your body. In Chinese medicine, the belief is that energy ("qi") can get blocked, leading to disease and other symptoms, so the placement of a microneedle in a meridian point stimulates the energy to flow once again, clearing the blockage and rebalancing the body.

EFT Tapping does much of the same, specifically for the brain and emotions—hence the name *Emotional* Freedom Technique. But no needles are needed—which is music to my ears since I personally opt out of needles every chance I get (something else to tap on!).

Instead, light tapping with your fingertips on key meridian points stimulates the flow of blocked energy, experienced as emotions. Emotions and energy are really one and the same. Sadness is energy. Joy is energy. When we are experiencing negative emotions or energetic blocks, EFT Tapping helps to stimulate the flow of energy and emotion, so that we can release the negative emotional response associated with beliefs, thoughts, and memories.

In the case of my test anxiety, my subconscious mind had internalized some funky falsehood about tests. I truly do not remember what it was— EFT Tapping is that effective at wiping it out, and I never experienced anxiety with tests again. But, as a result, the thought of the upcoming test was causing the same physiological response in my body every single time. My subconscious had marked it in red ink as a threat, and even though I was totally safe, I was having a very different subconscious reaction. The EFT Tapping session I did helped to release that anxiety and rebalance the energy within my body.

The research behind EFT Tapping shows that it has a staggering efficacy on health and mental health. In a 2019 study, a team of researchers tested 203 people who attended a four-day EFT workshop. During this study, they looked at various systems in the body: the central nervous system, which includes the brain and spinal cord; the circulatory system, which involves the heart and blood vessels; the endocrine system, which includes hormone levels; and the immune system. They also tracked psychological symptoms like anxiety and depression.

After just ONE workshop—sixty minutes of EFT Tapping—they performed detailed tests on thirty-one participants. An overview of what they found:

- 40 percent decline in anxiety
- 35 percent decline in depression
- 32 percent decline in post-traumatic stress disorder
- 57 percent decline in pain
- 74 percent decline in cravings

And all of these findings were "$P < .000$," a statistical metric that signifies that the observed result is so unlikely to have occurred by chance that it essentially rounds down to zero. In other words, there is an extremely low probability that the observed result is due to random variation alone.

What's more, happiness increased by 31 percent, $P = .000$, and salivary immunoglobulin A (SIgA), a critical antibody in saliva that's crucial for the body's immune system functionality, increased by 113 percent.

Significant improvements were also found in:

- Resting heart rate, which decreased by 8 percent with a $P = .001$
- Cortisol, the stress hormone, which decreased by 37 percent with a $P < .000$
- Systolic blood pressure, which decreased by 6 percent, $P = .001$
- Diastolic blood pressure, which decreased by 8 percent, $P < .000$

While this is my favorite study because it shows just how comprehensive the impact of EFT Tapping is, there are many other study findings that are absolutely worth noting here, such as these insights from a 2004 study by Joaquin Andrade, MD, and David Feinstein, PhD, that observed five thousand patients seeking treatment for anxiety over 5.5 years across eleven clinics:

- In the study, the patients received either cognitive behavioral therapy (CBT) with the option for medication when needed or EFT Tapping without medication. They would meet with an independent clinician who would interview the patient as the therapy began, then at month one, month three, month six, and one year into therapy. The findings were exciting. Sixty-three percent of the control group (the CBT with medication option) was judged as having improved by these independent clinicians, whereas 90 percent of the EFT Tapping group was judged as having improved.

- The study also showed how quickly the effects of EFT Tapping can take hold. Only three sessions of EFT Tapping were needed before the participant noticed a relief in their anxiety, whereas at least fifteen sessions of CBT were needed. EFT Tapping took *one-fifth* of the time.

- The study *also* illustrated how complete the relief from EFT Tapping can be. Whereas 51 percent of participants in the CBT group received complete relief from their anxiety symptoms, **76 percent** of EFT Tapping participants experienced complete relief.

And, it goes beyond emotions, as important as those are. Another one of the most fascinating pilot studies researched the difference in gene expression before and after EFT Tapping. This pilot study by M. E. Maharaj (2016) took place over only one, one-hour EFT Tapping session, and differential expression was found across seventy-two genes—from JUST ONE HOUR!

In the published study, the research team wrote that these were genes associated with:

- the suppression of cancer tumors
- protection against ultraviolet radiation
- regulation of type 2 diabetes insulin resistance
- immunity from opportunistic infections
- antiviral activity
- synaptic connectivity between neurons
- synthesis of both red and white blood cells
- enhancement of male fertility
- building white matter in the brain
- metabolic regulation
- neural plasticity
- reinforcement of cell membranes
- the reduction of oxidative stress

Overall, these biomarkers of EFT Tapping specifically reveal a decrease in stress and an increase in immunity. And while my own personal experience isn't quite "research," something fascinating I've noticed is I have barely gotten sick since I started regularly tapping five years ago.

But when I review the research, it makes sense—as much as I know I'm tapping for inner peace and the subconscious rewiring for uplevels, I'm also helping my body to build its strongest possible immune system.

I learned about EFT Tapping chiefly from my practitioner, coach, and mentor, Tiffany Jeffers—the hero who swooped in during my extra stuck phase and set me (and my nose) free. Tiffany discovered tapping for herself in her mid-thirties when she was also feeling extremely stuck. She was suffering from years of chronic pain, as well as PTSD from traumatic childhood experiences and serving in the military. A friend of hers told her about tapping, and she attended a live event to see what it was all about. As she began to tap, she shared that she could actually feel the physical pain start to dissolve from her body. She was shocked. She began to get one-on-one tapping sessions, and she was able to completely resolve her PTSD from all of her past experiences and move into a space that's called post-traumatic growth. This refers to a psychological space after PTSD that isn't just defined by bouncing back to one's pre-trauma state, but actually surpassing it and experiencing significant personal growth and resiliency.

Tapping also helped her to release financial blocks, relationship challenges, fears and phobias, and a radical number of physical health challenges to become completely medicine free. (Note: I'm not a doctor, and this is not a book about utilizing EFT Tapping to resolve medical challenges. I'm sharing this information to relay the profound shift in Tiffany's life. Please do not stop taking any medications without consulting with your doctor.) One of the best parts for Tiffany was how quickly it all shifted after years of talk therapy that had only helped a little. She was set free.

She fell in love with the work and trained for years to become an advanced EFT practitioner and life coach to help others and began her work volunteering at a long-term addiction and rehabilitation center called Habilitat, on the island of Oahu. She saw firsthand how tapping can completely transform even the toughest lives and watched clients find hope again and become their best through this work. She has offered one-on-one sessions for over a decade and now empowers high-performing professionals to crush mental blocks, find clarity and direction, release emotional baggage, and get personal and professional breakthroughs. She has been in a loving marriage for over two decades, and her family includes her two children and three dogs. Life feels very fulfilling and full of more joy than she ever thought possible. The power of tapping!

THE ORIGIN OF EFT TAPPING

The development of EFT Tapping as we know it is a highly fascinating story that speaks to the methodology's efficacy. The true origin is in Traditional Chinese Medicine and the meridian system, which is at the core of the modality of tapping. Rick Wilkes and Cathy Vartuli wrote a great story on how EFT Tapping was developed (see more in the Sources section), which includes the many layers of discovery that led to what's practiced today.

Roger Callahan, PhD, had been doing psychotherapy for thirty years and believed according to a confluence of Chinese medicine and cognitive behavioral therapy that emotional distress and psychological challenges were caused by disturbances in the energetic system of the body. He referred to these energetic systems as "thought fields." This is connected to Traditional Chinese Medicine, in which good health and emotional well-being are thought to be caused by an easy, natural flow of the qi within the body, along and through these pathways called meridians.

During his study of acupuncture, Callahan had a thought: What if just lightly tapping on these meridian points could also create a shift? He applied the theory on a patient named Mary who had a severe phobia of water—one that had haunted her since she was an infant. It was such a troublesome fear that she feared bathing, felt anxiety when it rained, and would have recurring nightmares about water. They had tried multiple psychotherapy alternatives to alleviate the fear over a year of their work together, to no avail. They would sit by his pool for water exposure, and she would leave the sessions with a splitting headache from the fear.

The way she explained the fear was an "awful feeling in the pit of her stomach." Drawing on his knowledge of the Chinese meridian system, Callahan knew that the meridian point located right underneath the eye was connected to the stomach. So, one day, he tried lightly tapping on this meridian point and others as she thought about her fear of water.

To both their shock, within minutes, her fear had completely and totally dissipated. All she felt was a calm relief when she thought about water, which excited her so much that she took off *running* toward his pool, feeling absolute exhilaration that the fear had now completely vanished. The fear NEVER returned—and all it took was a few quick minutes.

Since then, the EFT methodologies have expanded thanks to a few different pioneers. The true founder of EFT, who simplified and refined Roger Callahan's findings with Thought Field Therapy, is Gary Craig (who was a student of Callahan). He is a Stanford engineering graduate and life performance coach who was skeptical of tapping when he first heard about it. But he tried it with a few clients, who observed rapid and enormous inclines in well-being because of it, and he took it from there.

Craig's EFT Tapping is defined by mentally focusing upon a distressing issue, and then tapping lightly on the meridian points to release and dissolve the accompanying feelings. This is a type of EFT Tapping many are familiar with and is the type that I initially learned. Typically, this is done by following a script relevant to the issue at hand and tapping for several minutes, alternating between meridian points every thirty seconds or so.

FASTER EFT

The type of EFT Tapping that I've learned is specifically called Faster EFT, which is a variation of EFT that focuses on reprogramming the subconscious mind, and it was developed by Robert G. Smith. I personally find this technique to live up to its name—it's definitely faster and, in my opinion, more satisfying! Of course, always choose what works for you.

In standard EFT Tapping, the following meridian points are utilized:

- Top of the head
- Front of the eyebrow
- Side of the eye
- Underneath the eye
- Underneath the nose
- Chin
- Collarbone
- Side of the wrist, on the pinky finger side
- Squeezing the wrist, right underneath the palm of the hand

The process typically includes talking about one's feelings as one taps several times on each meridian point, moving through all the meridian points in the cycle until a shift is felt.

Faster EFT works differently. During a Faster EFT round of tapping, only the following meridian points are used:

- Front of the eyebrow
- Side of the eye
- Underneath the eye
- Collarbone
- Squeezing the wrist

These points were expertly selected for the Faster EFT process because each of them is thought to correspond with a specific element of release.

The front of the eyebrow point is especially helpful for deep emotional distress such as stress and anxiety, which is why it's a great first point to tap on in the sequence. In Chinese medicine, this point corresponds with the bladder, which is related to fight or flight. The first time I did a doorless helicopter ride as someone who's afraid of heights, I thought it would be a great way to see Manhattan! Although it was a gorgeous view and a total thrill, I'll never forget the acute feeling of being about to pee my pants whenever I'd try to turn my body to let my feet dangle out of the helicopter. I was shocked! I'd never had that type of physiological reaction—but I'd never been THAT HIGH in the sky before, secured by nothing except a seat belt. Anyway, believe me when I say the two are closely related.

The front of the eyebrow point is also helpful for headaches and tension in your upper body. For example, I carry a lot of tension in my neck and shoulders when I'm stressed, and lightly tapping on the front of the eyebrow is very helpful for this.

Then, the side of the eye point is great for releasing anger and resentment. In Chinese medicine, this is the meridian point associated with the gallbladder, which is also closely linked to the liver. These organs in our body are thought to hold irritation, anger, resentment, frustration, timidity, and indecisiveness. There can also be anxiety linked to this as well.

We often think of being "blinded" by rage, so this point is great for helping to calm and clear the mind. Tapping on it lightly can help to release feelings of confusion, fear of taking risks, and pent-up anger from past or present emotional experiences.

Underneath the eye is a great place to tap for worry and anxiety. In Chinese medicine, this meridian point is associated with the stomach. We're most prone to stomach issues when we're feeling fearful and anxious, and this is a great place to lightly tap to cause a shift and rebalance. A common sensation you may experience is a pit in your stomach. When you notice this, spend extra time tapping on this meridian point underneath the eye.

Finally, the collarbone point is a great tapping point to promote feelings of peace. When you lightly tap on it, it sends calming signals to the brain, which is why it's a powerful ending point to tap on. This is also usually the part of the tapping process where we state powerful affirmations out loud, and this works beautifully with the calming sensation.

In Chinese medicine, the collarbone point is associated with the kidneys, and sometimes the stomach as well. Tapping here can help with emotional regulation and infuse you with extra energy.

In addition to all that goodness, it's not *just* the actual act of tapping in Faster EFT that makes it so effective. Faster EFT combines the efficacy of the emotional release and energy rebalance achieved from tapping lightly on each meridian point *and* what's called a "pattern interrupt" between each round of tapping in order to rewire the brain.

Below is an example of this process in action. Imagine that you're worried about your end-of-year review meeting with your boss.

1. First, you would go to the emotion of the worry. How do you know you're worried? Answers tend to include that you get a nervous feeling in your chest, your heartbeat quickens, palms get sweaty, knees weak, arms are heavy (oops, that's Eminem).

2. You'd then close your eyes and really allow yourself to worry. Might as well! You've been worried this whole time. Then, ask yourself, *how* worried are you on a scale of 1–10? 10 is the most, nearly unbearable, and 1 is barely any at all.

3. You'd then start tapping on the four meridian points, spending about fifteen to thirty seconds on each. This is very light tapping. Imagining lightly tapping your fingertips on a keyboard when typing—just like that. Tapping harder won't make it work

faster! Let it be light and easy, finding a rhythm that feels good to you—not lightning fast, but not tortoise slow, either. You can't mess this up. Just let it feel good and be peaceful. We'll go over EFT scripts shortly, but what you say won't make or break this process.

4. After you've tapped on each meridian point, you'll squeeze your wrist, take a big deep breath in, then blow it out gently.

5. You'll then move into what's called a pattern interrupt (more on this in a second). This takes your brain totally off the topic of the worry, which weakens the neural pathway.

6. After the pattern interrupt, you will "go back and check it." You'll mentally pull up the distressing topic and any pictures, sounds, or emotions associated, then notice what's shifting. Rate the new feeling on your original scale of 1–10. After the first round of tapping, you may feel it more, feel it less, feel something different, or even experience NO shift. It can take a second—but after a few rounds of tapping, you should notice a clear, measurable difference.

Pattern Interrupts

Tapping on its own is HIGHLY effective, but pattern interrupts are my favorite part of the entire process to achieve shifts even more quickly. This is because when the brain is thinking about something that causes it distress, it's very difficult for it to break out of that pattern. You've definitely experienced this when you've been too worried about something to fall asleep at night. You'd really prefer to just relax, trust the process, surrender it . . . but the worry creates an endless cycle of ruminating thoughts. Or maybe you've been worried about something all day long, so it just feels best to tell everyone and their mother about it, get their take, talk it out, Google it, consult a psychic and maybe book a random tarot reading through social media, and go over every contingency plan.

This is your brain's way of trying to keep you safe. When there's a problem at hand, it does not want to rest until the problem is solved. But in the case of *worry*, especially when it's worrying about something out of our hands or something that's not happening until the end of the month, there's nothing to be done. But your subconscious mind does not know this. The worry is a response to a perceived threat.

And the worry itself is distressing, too, so the continued worry is actually further evidence and proof to the subconscious that *more* worrying is needed. It creates worry MOMENTUM! This is why a pattern interrupt is deeply impactful. When the brain is tugged off the worry swiftly and promptly and onto something totally different, it signals to the brain that the worry isn't as important as it appeared to be. This prunes the neural pathway of worry.

Examples of pattern interrupts can include:

- Immediately shifting gears and thinking about your favorite vacation you've ever been on
- Getting up and doing three jumping jacks
- Counting everything in the room around you that's pink
- Listening to your favorite happy song and dancing
- Taking a few minutes to tidy up your room
- Texting a friend back about a totally different topic
- Thinking about how many cities you can name that start with the letter *B*
- Replaying, in great detail, a bite of that delicious tiramisu you tasted last week

In my Dreamaway ninety-minute EFT Tapping and subconscious breakthrough sessions, I always go the extra mile with these pattern interrupts between the rounds of tapping. It could be anything from getting up to stand on one foot and spell your name backwards to thinking about how you'd explain the taste of water to someone who's never tried it. With so many options, a good rule of thumb is to match the type of pattern interrupt with the way the emotion is impacting you.

If you feel emotions in your body as a sensation, it's important to get up and *move* between rounds of tapping. Do jumping jacks. Dance. Touch your toes. Walk around the room. Tickle your kneecaps or elbows. You can also shake your body. Humans are actually the only mammals that do not necessarily shake after a traumatic event. Other animals will physically shake after something stressful happens—this allows their nervous system to reset and release any embodied tension. So, quite literally get up and shake it like a Polaroid picture! No one is watching, so just be silly and figure out what "shaking" looks like to you.

If you're clearing or healing something you visibly see, such as a vivid memory or an abstract mental image, pattern interrupt by imagining something so wild and different. Like a brown bear dancing on a table in a club to "In da Club" because he had orange juice for the first time and he has a sugar rush. Or a beaver trying on lipstick shades and accidentally getting swipes of them all on his big two front buck teeth. You can also watch something; I love to queue up some funny videos if I'm tapping on my own. Major recommendation: news bloopers on YouTube. You could even watch one of your favorite lighthearted shows for just a few minutes before you go back and check the original emotion.

If you're clearing something you hear, like you can actually hear the upsetting words someone said to you, try playing some music. One of my favorite pattern interrupts is banjo music. It's just so lighthearted; it's very challenging to stay focused on the cause of the negative emotion when that sweet banjo is plucking away and conjuring up images of life on the farm and cute barnyard animals.

We're about to get in depth on how to use tapping to rewire your subconscious mind, but for the sake of giving it a whirl right now, let's do something really easy together and just tap on something small that's bothering you. Key word here: SMALL. This could be some dread for your workout later, annoyance over a minor comment a friend said the other day, or not knowing what to wear to that work presentation next week. We'll save the bigger fish for later.

Once you pinpoint what that is, ask yourself, *How do I know this is bothering me?* With small irritations, it can be through small sensations in your body. Maybe your neck feels tense. There's a little pit in your stomach. Or you just feel "annoyed," even if you don't know how to explain it.

Close your eyes and *be* with the emotion. Let it bother you! The funny thing about humans is we usually either let something bother us in the background or cause a big stir about it by devoting a ton of mental attention and energy to it. We'll talk about it with our friends or our partner. We'll scoff at it. But we seldom sit in the emotion of the matter and just let ourselves *feel* it.

We aren't going to stay in this feeling though; don't worry. When we allow ourselves to fully feel something, we are squarely in that neural pathway. This might not show up as a feeling for you; you may see something—like an image of the gym, if you're dreading working out, or even a big black blob of dread. You also might hear something, like your friend saying that comment, or even circus music! Whatever it is, all you need to do at first is be present with it. Insert self-awareness by observing "how you know." Because you *do* know this bothers you. And your body has a unique way of making that felt.

Then, ask yourself how much it's bothering you on a scale of 1–10.

You'll then start tapping.

Lightly tap on the front of your eyebrow, as you list out loud all of the feelings, sights, and sounds associated. State, "This is really bothering me."

Go ahead and continue here and let yourself verbally express the hardest parts.

It might sound like "I'm just so annoyed. Ugh! I'm dreading this so much."

Move your tapping to the side of your eye, and state out loud as you continue tapping something like "I'd rather let this go. It feels difficult to let this go, but maybe, just maybe, I can return to a space of peace around this. It's safe to let this dissolve and evaporate."

Then, tap underneath your eye, as you say, "As I let this go, everything feels better, and lighter. I feel free! It's safe to experience freedom and peace from this. Maybe I can choose a new feeling and a new story. I don't need to hold on to this in order to stay safe."

Finally, tap on your collarbone point, as you say, "I am ready to feel better than ever before. Releasing this is so easy. I choose to love my life. I choose to see this differently. I let peace and joy flood my being. I'm ready to let this go."

Squeeze either wrist, take a big deep breath in, and imagine gently blowing out any remaining frustration with your exhale.

Then I want you to actually stand up and do three jumping jacks. Right now. Go do it. I don't care if you're in public. Okay, fine, if you're in public, you can do a little jumping jack in your chair. Fake it. Just move your body.

Then, I want you to close your eyes and think about a really happy memory in a happy place. See all the sights, hear all the sounds, and allow yourself to feel the good feelings. Transport yourself to this moment in time as if it's actually happening right now. Don't let up until you actually create a good feeling from the reflection, whether it's peace or glee or a little giggle remembering something silly that happened in the memory.

Squeeze either wrist again and take a big deep breath in, inhaling even more peace and good energy, and exhale into a space of relief.

Now, you'll "go back and check it." This means you're checking the original emotion that felt bothersome to you. Has it changed? Wherever you are with it—whether it's stayed the same, gone up, gone down, or completely disappeared—is perfect. This is a process. Small bothers are traditionally easier to clear, but I like to say that all limiting beliefs or emotions are like layers of an onion.

Maybe something that felt small to you in the moment, like that annoying thing your friend said, is actually part of a much deeper story— because it reminded you of something your brother would always say to you or triggered a feeling you had at your old job when you never felt you were doing enough. We'll get more into this in the upcoming chapter on how to REWIRE, but what's important for you to know and recognize for now is that any shift is major, and being present with your thoughts and feelings is critically important. (And as always, if you uncover something much bigger, please work one-on-one with a trained practitioner or a licensed counselor. Healing isn't meant to be done alone.)

If you're "neutral," i.e., you feel totally clear, GREAT! But it's very possible that you'll need a few rounds to clear a small bother if it's your first time. So you'd just go back and repeat the process I just took you through.

Hacks for Major Transformation in a Few Tapping Rounds

1. **When in doubt, amp up the pattern interrupts.** The act of tapping is tremendously powerful for releasing emotions and regulating your nervous system; you may immediately feel peace the second your fingers begin to tippy-tap-dance on the meridian points! It's always going to be a necessary part of the process. However, I've found that I've gotten the BIGGEST, most IMMEDIATE shifts when I've had a big pattern interrupt. Go ahead and review the list of potential pattern interrupts for this! This can absolutely be achieved on your own, especially with how much you can make yourself laugh, shake out the energy, or focus on something else entirely. You'll find what works for you.

I will add that this is made MUCH easier when you're working one-on-one with a practitioner, because when a third party can pattern interrupt you when you're less inclined to distract yourself—e.g., when you're deep in the bothersome "Ugh I simply cannot believe she said that, who does she think she is, why I oughta, GRR, I should've said this back, maybe I should text her right n—" and they hit you with a *BANJO MUSIC, GET UP AND DANCE LIKE A GRIZZLY BEAR AT THE RODEO!*— you'd be shocked at just how much can shift very, very quickly.

2. **What you say is not as important as the actual process.** Many times, people get hung up on the perfect tapping script. In my experience, it doesn't really matter what you say. As a rule of thumb, I like to begin with stating out loud how much something is bothering me, to let myself express it. On mainly the first two tapping points of front of the eyebrow and side of the eye, I'll let myself vent! But by the time I get to underneath the eye and the collarbone, I want to make sure I'm saying things like, "It's safe to let this go. It's safe to believe in something new." I also like to state out loud what I'd rather believe or experience.

Technically, you could just tap and say out loud, "It's safe to let this go" on every tapping point and still get the same shifts. Or, to give a very different example, I used to tap while coming up with a funny animal story on each point. This is a silly idea my mom came up with, a pattern interrupt within a tapping script, so to speak.

An example:

Front of the eyebrow: "There's a cute little corgi at the McDonald's drive-thru, ordering a milkshake!"

Side of the eye: "Now there's a hippo putting on a yellow polka-dot bow tie for his school picture!"

Underneath the eye: "Ah yes, now a kangaroo wearing an apron and hosting a cooking show on how to make Brussels sprouts with candied pecans."

Collarbone: "Silly silly moose struttin' to the beat as he walks to work with his headphones over his antlers."

Squeeze wrist, deep breath in, blow it out gently.

You'd be amazed how much even something like that can help—and you can just come up with it on your own! You can also weave your own story entirely while tapping, where you speak out loud a ridiculous, silly story while spending twenty seconds tapping on each of the four meridian points in sequence.

Here are some prompts to get you started:

- A beaver who JUST learned about the tooth fairy and is convinced one of his big front teeth will earn him the jackpot

- A cheetah who has opted for a rest day and is trying to do a slow, leisurely walk through the park with his best friend the sloth, but his paws are twitching with the urge to run really, really fast

- A basset hound who mistakenly enters a yoga class for cats only, but they are happy to have him, and the instructor has to make sure his paws don't land on his long basset hound ears with all the yoga poses

- A raccoon who starts a "Trash Treasure" blog and reviews local trash cans for the best treasures on his viral social media page

Take these prompts and pretend you're telling a small child a bedtime story. Let your imagination run wild. Let yourself giggle. The rapid shift from REALLY feeling and thinking about what's bothering you to tapping and speaking out loud a story of an ambitious giraffe hosting a leaf-tasting tour or a grizzly bear who discovered his affinity for baking fluffy, flaky croissants will rapidly change your life. Even if that's the silliest, most random thing you've ever read in a "self-help" book. Hey, you can't knock what works!

I strongly recommend you begin your foray into tapping with a few moments throughout your day when you're feeling worried or bothered, to illustrate to yourself how it works. We're always going for relief here. If something no longer bothers you as much as it did, that's huge! Peace is always the answer.

CHAPTER REVIEW AND EXERCISES
TL;DR

• EFT Tapping has a rapidly growing body of research backing its astounding efficacy. You're on the cutting edge of some major life changes!

• You can tap at any time using the meridian points of the front of the eyebrow, side of the eye, underneath the eye, and the collarbone. Then, squeeze your wrist and take a big, deep breath in.

• One of the most critical steps of the process is the PATTERN INTERRUPT! The sillier, the better.

• Match the pattern interrupt to the type of disturbance. If you feel something physically, dance or shake it out. If you hear something, turn on funny music—and if you see something in your mind's eye, let it melt away like watercolors turning into a gorgeous sunset. Or, just add a camel loudly crunching carrots to the memory and see how that shakes it up.

Set Yourself Free

Now that you've learned how to tap, you're ready to set yourself free when needed! Throughout today or this week, notice if anything comes up that bothers you. Impatience in traffic, stress about a looming work deadline, even icky, sticky exhaustion despite your nine hours of sleep and big coffee.

Close your eyes and go into your body. Notice how you know it's bothering you. Feelings, sights, sounds—we have to identify it to clear it.

Begin your tapping rounds!

Front of the eyebrow: State out loud exactly how you're feeling and how you know it bothers you.

Side of the eye: Let yourself vent a little more, say UGH!

Underneath the eye: Simply say, "It's safe to let this go. Maybe, just maybe, everything is always working out for me." Say this as many times as it feels good to you.

Collarbone: Add in a dose of what you'd rather believe, or speak out loud about what is going well in your life. Continue with "it's safe to let this go, it's safe to feel peace" as it feels good to you.

Squeeze your wrist, take a big deep breath in, and blow it out gently.

Then, close your eyes and imagine you're back at your favorite vacation place. Dial up the good feelings from the weather, the food, the company, where you stayed, the fun agenda, the vibe of this amazing location.

Then, stand up and have a dance party as if you're doing a happy dance back at that vacation spot! Woohoo!

You can then close your eyes and picture whatever you're stressed about working out perfectly. What do you want to have happen from here? Let it play out in your mind's eye as a quick mind movie, and play it several times.

Then, "go back and check it." Notice any shifts. How does it feel? Do this again as many times as you'd like, experimenting with pattern interrupts and which verbal affirmations make you feel best.

CHAPTER 6

HOW TO USE EFT TO REWIRE

O f course, beyond using it for immediate relief if we're nervous about an upcoming interview or feeling down about a missed opportunity, we want to know how to alter our reality using EFT Tapping. This, my friends, is where the transformation *really* begins. And since you've come this far, you actually already know so much that will lend itself to this beautifully.

If you review your journaling on your subconscious breakthrough questions, you'll likely see that you've stumbled across many memories, thought fragments, words spoken to you, or archetypal feelings from your life that have kept you stuck. You may have unpacked some major fears that live beneath the surface in your subconscious. And for all of them, I imagine some feelings came up to the surface.

You may be the type of person who feels emotions acutely. This is me! I feel everything very, very deeply. I am immediately aware if I'm feeling sad, anxious, or angry—I'm well-versed in the Emotional Dictionary.

Not everyone is like this, though, so if you don't feel in touch with your emotions, fear not. It could also come up for you as a sensation, such as becoming aware of tension in your neck or the feeling of a pit in your stomach as you remember a past memory related to the subconscious block at hand.

Here are some other physical sensations that could arise, indicating that your subconscious is bothered by a memory:

• Heart rate quickening
• Headache
• Chest tightness

• Getting hot, or getting cold
• Butterflies in the stomach
• Feeling lightheaded
• A sense of unease

Truly, don't discount any feeling that could arise. A strange dull pain in your left rib? We'll take it! Tingling in your right palm? Perfect! We trust that the subconscious is presenting to us that something is amiss. We can now use this feeling to carry us home and help us release.

If you don't feel anything at all, physical or emotional, there's still no reason to worry. Many of us are highly visual. If you can see the memory, or even see a symbolic, abstract image associated with it (like a big black hole, or an orange pickup truck—it can be as random or as poignant as either of those), this too is the subconscious presenting how it's processing information.

You also could hear something, like the words that were stated to you or sounds from a specific incident.

We want to ease the subconscious mind, which means we need to use these reactions to guide us.

Here's an example of how this could play out, rewiring-style.

Imagine that Anita is feeling very lonely and heavily blocked in love. She seems to only attract partners who do not want a relationship—but of course, they always seem to decide this after she catches feelings. This pattern has been recurring so many times that she's had enough. So, she goes through the subconscious breakthrough process to figure out what the heck is going on.

As she journals on "What bad thing might happen if you meet your person and begin a happy relationship?" she immediately gets struck by a memory of her high school partner who was one year older than her. They had a wonderful six months together, and it was her true first love.

She believed she would marry him and became very aware of these feelings a few months into the relationship—at the same time that he was hearing back from the colleges he applied to. And that's when it happened. He found out he got into his dream school on the other side of the country. Suddenly, their relationship felt like a ticking time bomb. Every moment of happiness had an underlying melancholy. She'd be happy at dinner with him, then feel a sadness set in on the way home: they were on borrowed time. In a few months, he was moving. After many months of these interwoven feelings of great bliss and deep sadness, they called it quits, knowing long distance was too much for them at that time.

Now, it's a decade later, and her subconscious has held tightly this entire time to this upsetting experience. The belief: "Love is pain. It cannot last. And while you have it, you will have to constantly be worried about the inevitable end."

WHEW! No wonder it's getting blocked! It's her big "No wonder!"

You may think, "Well, Anita WANTS a committed relationship. It's just the people she's choosing to date who don't. It's THEIR choice."

Okay, true. But why do we think she's choosing them? It certainly isn't conscious. She isn't thinking to herself, "You know what sounds great? Let me invest even more time, energy, and hope into someone who ultimately isn't going to want the same commitment I do."

Doesn't this seem to be concocted beautifully by the subconscious, which is simply repeating old, familiar patterns of behavior and experience since that's all it knows? Her conscious efforts are well-intentioned and aligned with what she wants. But as we know, that's only 5 percent of the story.

Her subconscious is making sure that can't happen again, because the threat is too immense. It's recycling the old story of the high school boyfriend again and again and again as a warning sign. Her subconscious does not know that it could ever be another way; this isn't how it works.

It got the input from this memory: LOVE IS PAINFUL. And it wants to keep Anita safe. Safety = not getting into any relationship that involves commitment.

As Anita finds this memory, it's a light bulb. It makes it all make sense. Now, it's time to neutralize the intense emotional reaction associated with the memory. In other words, it's time to scrub the red ink off its file in the file folder, so the subconscious can just chill and allow a beautiful happily-ever-after story, please and thank you very much.

Here's how the process will work now:

1. Anita will close her eyes and go into the memory of her high school boyfriend. There are likely many memories that come up, and she can give them each a label. Perhaps there's the one when he committed to the out-of-state school, the one where she cried after prom, and the one of the final breakup.

2. For each of these memories, she is going to notice how she KNOWS it bothers her. Maybe her eyes sting with tears. Maybe she feels a tightness in her chest. Maybe she sees his text delivering the news. Maybe she sees his face in the moment of their breakup, or something extremely random, like the way the lamp reflected light onto the wall of her bedroom the night she sat in silence for hours, processing that her heart was about to be broken. These are fragments of information that the subconscious clings to as proof and evidence for the belief.

3. She will then start tapping on one memory at a time. She does this by pulling up the memory and emotion as much as possible and asking herself how much she can feel it on a scale of 1–10.

4. Throughout the rounds of tapping, she can state the feeling and what she would rather believe. (More on this from a Neuro-Linguistic Programming perspective momentarily!) She makes sure to include effective pattern interrupts in between the rounds of tapping—she gets up and shakes it out, she watches a funny video, she quickly unloads the dishwasher while listening to a voice

memo from a friend, she remembers the best part of her trip to Maine last summer and the way the sea breeze brought her peace.

5. She "goes back and checks it" each time, noticing what changes. Maybe new related memories will appear. But as she goes, one thing is for certain: the strong emotions/sensations/visuals/ sounds associated with the memories begin to fade.

6. She can now also get a head start on building out NEW neural pathways by making up mind movies of what she would rather believe and experience. In her case, a love in which it's safe, it's constant, and it can actually work out and unfold beautifully with no end in sight. They meet, they feel the same, they commit, they're great partners to one another and plan for a life together. And that life just gets better and better and better. She makes this visual as specific as possible, down to the small moments like lying on the couch together at night watching their favorite show, and the big moments, like dancing the night away at their tenth anniversary party, surrounded by their family and friends, to "Best of My Love."

Over the course of this process, her subconscious lets down its guard. Here's what happens: Whenever she previously thought of the memory, it usually came up with a boatload of emotions, leading the subconscious into a frenzy of "MUST AVOID AT ALL COSTS IN THE FUTURE!" Now, however, she just feels peace. She feels hope for a new future. Her subconscious mind is okay with all of it.

Which means it no longer throws up any alarm bells or Red Ink file folders next time she meets someone she could commit to. Instead, it has future evidence—from her great mind movie work—on how good and safe the whole thing could be. And because it's no longer stuck on any information or memories to the contrary, it's at peace with a new beginning.

Now, this doesn't mean she has amnesia. She can still remember everything. But it's about her emotional reaction to the memories. She can be at peace after this process, feeling grateful for the chapter of her life and all she learned. But she does not need to hold on to the heart-break to move forward safely.

The Power of Dissolving Neural Pathways

The real beauty of Faster EFT—beyond, of course, bringing incredible relief—is this power of neuroplasticity, which is the brain's ability to rewire itself. Neuroplasticity essentially just means that the brain has the ability to change. You now know all about neural pathways and how every neural pathway in your brain is devoted to a core belief or memory. The more "evidence" for this belief system, the thicker the neural pathway.

In Anita's case, she had a neural pathway devoted to the belief that love is pain. And the greatest evidence her subconscious had for this was her high school boyfriend. Through tapping and neutralizing the emotional response, her neural pathway for this belief was weakened, if not totally dissolved.

Many times, subconscious work really is this logical. There was one main memory that the subconscious derived meaning from, and clearing it opened up a brand-new way of being.

But we are complex beings who have had many different unique experiences. We have witnessed a great deal, learned a great deal. We've watched movies and TV shows, read books, seen friends and family go through their own life events, and heard them tell us things that stuck with us. Where there is one strong subconscious belief, there is usually a great deal of related memories, experiences, thoughts, emotions, and feelings associated with it. Which means we may need to work on a belief from multiple angles, multiple times. Each one produces a shift in our feelings and our reality, so fear not. But it's important to know that one element is likely attached to more.

I like to think of the brain's neural pathways as a big ball of tangled yarn. This isn't to dismiss the awesome power of the brain by simplifying it, but rather to illustrate just how interconnected so many of our neural pathways are. The best part of this work is uncovering just what those are, and what is unexpectedly knotted together.

To illustrate this, think about the last time you smelled or tasted something that unlocked a core memory you had long forgotten. In the great film *Ratatouille* (sorry, potential spoiler alert here!), the food critic tries the ratatouille dish and is immediately transported to being a young boy, eating his mother's ratatouille. We see it played out beautifully on the screen: his widened eyes as the taste unexpectedly evokes such a powerful memory; it's almost like he took a time machine back into his past. (Didn't I tell you putting things in childlike terms could be an effective shortcut?)

The same is true of thoughts, tastes, smells, sounds, and visual triggers. I've noticed I really don't like listening to certain songs that were popular during challenging times of my life, like a OneRepublic song that was constantly on the radio during my breakup with my first love. It's just a song, yet it triggers the neural pathway related to a time long, long ago, and when I hear it I can actually feel the remnants of the heartbreak.

This is important because as you begin your journey to identify your core beliefs, you may stumble across some memories or mental pictures that don't seem to "make sense" in the context of what you're working on. I once worked with an athlete who kept falling short of the personal record necessary to qualify for the Olympics, and as we went deeper in the subconscious discovery, she kept seeing the mental image of one of her teammates, which was very confusing. Upon further consideration, we realized that her subconscious had somehow conflated her fear of making the Olympics with the fear of disappointing or leaving behind her teammate, because there were limited spots available on the team.

There have been times that as I've closed my eyes and gone into a feeling, a random mental picture will come up that doesn't seem to make sense at all. I just trust that somehow, the neural pathway of whatever I'm tapping on has become entangled with an early memory that is held in place by this mental image. There's no need to figure out what it is; I can just clear it using tapping and a few other techniques, as we'll get into in depth in the next chapter.

The power of tapping is in sorting out the tangled yarn of the neural pathways. Remember, every neural pathway is held in place by beliefs and accompanying emotions. Imagine that someone named Margaret has been struggling with a belief that it's exceedingly difficult to make it as an actor and land a role on TV. In fact, maybe she's even decided it's never going to happen for her, even though she keeps auditioning.

There are many neural pathways in the "yarn ball" of her brain devoted to evidence of this, and the evidence comes with accompanying emotions. As examples, some of these neural pathways could include:

• Unhealed heartbreak about past rejections for parts she really, really wanted.

• Unhealed perceptions on an ideal career from what she witnessed in her parents' careers.

• Some funky worthiness wounds that have made her believe she isn't worthy of being a serious TV actress, perhaps because of things that have been said to her or other false internalizations.

Imagine that Margaret's best friend lands a major part on a TV show, and when she FaceTimes her to tell her the news, Margaret's stomach drops, tears come to her eyes, and she feels ... incredible discomfort. She pushes through the tears, puts on her best happy face, and says congratulations a hundred times, all while mentally shaming herself for not being happy for her best friend. As she gets off the call, she racks her brain for how and why she would have that reaction. She argues with herself mentally, immediately in a tug-of-war about her perception about how she should have reacted and why she did react that way.

But it makes sense. If there weren't other neural pathways tangled up in this, Margaret *would* solely feel happiness for her friend—because it wouldn't mean anything about *her*. But so much more is going on beneath the surface. This news was like salt in the wound of Margaret's past rejections, the unhealed perceptions of her parents, and her worthiness issues. All of these past experiences and traumas were activated by the trigger because they're interlocked in the tangled neural pathways. But there's a gift in this—Margaret now can face all her "No wonder!"s. The poet Rumi said, "The wound is the place where the light enters you." I also like to think of this light as a flashlight, illuminating the troves of the subconscious mind where limiting beliefs and blocks have been lying dormant, running the show. Sometimes, an external trigger is the offset that leads to the greatest transformation.

What Margaret can now do is tap on every relevant past experience and "No wonder!" and as the emotion neutralizes, it will work to dissolve the neural pathway devoted to it. This weakens the original belief system that she isn't good enough to be a TV actress, and with a healthy dose of NEW belief integration—such as a visualization of the best it could be in the future, down to landing a big part, filming on set, and walking the red carpet—the ball of tangled yarn slowly begins to untangle itself and create more cohesion, which will allow Margaret to feel genuinely happy for her best friend without the impulse, knee-jerk, subconscious reaction of the pain and worry about her own career and dreams. In fact, maybe she can even see it as evidence that if it's happening for someone so close to her, that must mean it's possible for her as well.

And that's the goal: peace. For your thought process and navigation through this world to feel easy and happy, rather than akin to traversing mental minefields. Imagine if your nervous system could stay regulated and your hopes could stay high regardless of the triggers that get under your skin or keep you up at night. Imagine if you could have FEWER triggers—even in areas of your life that have really bothered you for a long, long time. This isn't to say that you'll ever reach a place where you're peachy and coasting every single minute of the rest of your life, but I can tell you wholeheartedly from personal experience that you will feel SO much better, and now always have a tool to help you when the inevitable struggles arise. *This* is the goal and solution of EFT Tapping, and what I've found to be true time and time again.

DISSOLVING ONE DISSOLVES OTHERS

One of my clients, Charlotte, did one of my tapping sessions focused on helping participants heal and release memories that have made them doubt their worthiness. Something wild happened just hours later.

Her ex-situationship, who had done a number on her perception of her worthiness many years prior, randomly called to apologize for his behavior! He was very clear that his actions were not about her at all, but rather his own inability to commit at that time because of his own issues. What . . . the *heck*?

She hadn't even been tapping about him—just a feeling related to him. Which shows how interlinked our brain's neural pathways are!

There may be other times you're tapping to clear one main belief or memory and suddenly another that you didn't even know was related flashes in your mind. It's so important to trust the process, with total and complete acceptance for all of it. Look at what comes up through the lens of curiosity. This goes back to the subconscious breakthrough question "When in the past did you also feel this way?" In other words, what does this remind you of?

In order to be as efficient as possible in finding the source, I recommend you go back as far into the past as possible when you start tapping. The reason for this is because of how neural pathways are formed. It's commonly thought of in Faster EFT as a tree analogy.

There is the "root cause" of the block or fear—this is where it all began. This is the initial experience. The memory that carries the real punch emotionally. The first moment you started to internalize a false belief.

And remember, the RAS got to work really quickly, seeking to confirm this initial belief and experience with MORE evidence. Confirmation bias kicked in. This has formed the entire tree, and all the branches—your entire life since that initial root experience. All the ways it's infiltrated other areas of your life. All the similar experiences.

For example, imagine that as you're free-writing in your journal on your "No wonder!"s about healthy romantic love, you stumble across an early childhood memory about your father being out of town for long periods of time for work. You remember and recognize that familiar feeling of abandonment, and it feels connected to your adult experiences in love. Bingo. No wonder!

Well, now as an adult, you could easily have had a recent experience of a partner who kept leaving you emotionally desolate by retreating into their career repeatedly for days at a time without so much as a text or call. You *could* tap on the worst parts of that memory—and you should. But, effectively, this recent experience is a tree branch of the overall tree of the feeling of abandonment. Releasing the branch *does* provide relief and make a difference, but you know what would be a complete and total paradigm shift?

Clearing it from the *root*. Which means clearing the earliest possible memory you have—in this case, the experience of a commonly absent father who put work travels above all else. When you tap on the initial experience, it weakens the other neural pathways, even dissolving them from beneath.

You may feel the sting of your recent heartbreak more than the pain your five-year-old self felt, but it's all connected. It always amazes clients when we start at the root, then I ask them to go back and check their emotional response to the recent situation. It's *always* less. This will give you a big leg up in your rewiring journey. When in doubt, GO TO THE ROOT.

This is far more effective than playing a game of Whac-A-Mole with tons of memories and experiences that have happened since. If you can't remember the root memory, that is OKAY. Go back as far as you can. Even if it's just a feeling or a picture that doesn't have a clear conscious story attached, TRUST IT. Tap. The goal is peace.

USE NLP ON YOURSELF

Another powerful way of dissolving neural pathways is understanding how they're held in place by *language*. We are all communicators! Insert Neuro-Linguistic Programming, or NLP, which you can think of as a manual for your mind. NLP helps us to understand how our thoughts, behavior, and words are interconnected. I especially like to use this with language, because how we communicate and describe our feelings and experiences is like getting a key to the subconscious mind. This is a very easy, straightforward hack to understand your brain better and target limiting beliefs and blocks as you tap.

Imagine that you're talking to a friend and they're confiding in you how hard it's been for them to pay off debt. As they talk, they're using very specific language. "I feel like I just can't get out from under it, and it's just building up and up and up," they say. "It makes me feel small and stressed and panicked."

Essentially, everything they just said can work for NLP. Their words created a very clear picture. If you were to recommend that they tap, you should also recommend that they use those exact words out loud as they do.

In your journaling, there are likely some key words and phrases that you find you've used numerous times. There also tend to be metaphors that arise when we journal because the subconscious operates in metaphors and symbols. Especially in response to the question "How would you describe this to a small child?" Some metaphors may include:

• It feels like I run into a concrete wall.

• I'm trying to walk uphill.

• I'm crushed under the weight of it.

• There's an elephant on my chest.

• I am reaching and grasping, but it's always just out of reach.

• It feels like sand slipping through my fingers.

• I feel like I'm standing naked and exposed onstage.

• I feel like I'm banging on a door but no one comes to open it.

The options here are endless, and it's always very interesting to see what it is for you. Know this: these are subconscious statements. The words that the subconscious uses are very important for the sake of rewiring. You can use these words as you tap, because as you do, it tugs on the associated neural pathway.

RELEASING IMAGES

You may also see an abstract mind image of one of these statements, such as the door that won't open or the hand reaching for something just out of reach. You can release this image with the following easy visualizations:

- Imagine putting the image in a snow globe, then shaking the snow globe and watching the snow turn everything to white.

- Imagine putting the image up on a dry-erase board, then wiping it away, clean and satisfying.

- Imagine putting the image in a softball and batting it into space, where it lands among the stars.

- Imagine a squirrel coming over with a hair dryer and pointing it at the image, heating it up so much that it starts to melt away and all that's left is the squirrel's proud reflection in the mirror.

Get creative here, and remember that after every visual shift, you want to pattern interrupt. So, after you see that visual process, close your eyes and think of the most beautiful sunset you've ever seen or replay a scene in your mind from your favorite movie. You can then "go back and check it" and repeat it as much as possible.

CHAPTER REVIEW

TL;DR

In sum, there are many ways to dissolve neural pathways, and your most important takeaways should be:

• EFT Tapping to dissolve emotions and associated energy. When in doubt, tap. Tap, tap, tap! You'll feel a shift in real time, truly within minutes. Make sure you're employing the pattern interrupts to get even faster shifts.

• To clear a belief or pattern effectively, go back to the root. Go back as far as you can go, even if you can't see the entire memory or fully understand it. Then, tap on that.

• Trust all the ways a neural pathway can reveal itself. Work with the stated or journaled words and repeat them out loud while tapping. See if images are associated and melt them away. Notice feelings and dance them out. And always remember to insert the GOOD in between. I can't harp on the pattern interrupts enough—this step helps immensely in rewiring the brain, because it builds out new and different neural pathways. Which is what the next chapter is all about.

CHAPTER 7

BUILDING NEW NEURAL PATHWAYS

So, we know that tapping helps us to release and dissolve neural pathways, but it's also important what we build out in terms of the *new* beliefs. This chapter will dive into how we can build out positive, inspiring neural pathways for what we'd rather believe. These exercises can be done while tapping or as an ancillary, rewiring-supporting activity.

NLP, Yet Again

In the last chapter, you learned how your initial expression of how you feel is representative of your brain's linguistic programming. We can use this for building new neural pathways, too, based on how the brain already understands information. In essence, this is how we can put new affirmations and statements in terms your brain can understand. There are a few ways to do this.

1. **For a total belief reversal, ask yourself what the OPPOSITE of a negative statement is.** If you constantly feel like money is slipping through your fingers like sand, what would the opposite picture or linguistic representation be? This may feel like a mental challenge or riddle, but remember, it doesn't have to be a perfect opposite. It doesn't need to be about sand at all, in this case. Reduced to the heart of the matter, how would you know and feel that money was actually something you handled well, could hold on to, and was something that felt secure? Maybe it could feel like a sturdy vault? Or like the ocean, that always has the same depths throughout the seasons and changing weather? These are just ideas—it's important to see what *your* brain produces. So, first ask yourself how you'd describe your block or problem to a

small child. See the key words and phrases. See the key metaphors or images. Then, reverse it. If it feels *hopeless*, a new word could be . . . *hopeful*? If it feels *challenging*, a new word could be *easy*. It's quite easy!

2. **How would you describe it to a friend if the belief was totally rewired?** We can also do a little make believe that we've waved a magic wand and the initial belief causing the block is yesterday's news. In its place is a far more empowering belief, and your life looks completely different. Flash forward to one month or one year in the future, whatever feels right. Imagine you're catching up with a friend over lunch or even writing me a note to share what's changed. How would you describe your new life? How does it feel? How do you know a shift has occurred?

For example, imagine that Cooper is having a really difficult time speaking up at work during meetings. It started when he got his promotion and began attending important board meetings alongside more senior staff members. He has ideas to share, but when the opportunities to do so present themselves, he feels a throat tightness and butterflies and can't seem to raise his hand or get the words out. I'd ask Cooper what it would look like and feel like in a month or two when this feeling and fear released. Maybe he would say to a friend who asked how work was going, "I speak up when I have ideas. I speak clearly. I feel secure and confident and grounded in the moment. I feel my chair supporting me, and I'm amazed at how intelligent I sound as I express myself! It's received well and I'm making a name for myself, and I see my higher-ups smiling and nodding proudly as I speak."

Wow, doesn't that sound and feel great (if a little detailed for a casual question from a friend)? Now Cooper knows what to say as he taps and what exactly to envision for his mind movies. It's important to note, these words would be unique to Cooper. Someone else could be having the same issue at work and want to seek out the same feelings of confidence and flow but use totally different words and imagery to describe the moment. You know your own brain best.

Contact with Your Future Self

My all-time favorite hack for building new neural pathways is communication with my future self. I implement many future-self mind movies in the tapping sessions I host as a result. The principle is that we all have future versions of ourselves who are still very much *us*, but they're living on the other side of this block, fear, and limiting belief. They've smashed that "No wonder!" to smithereens and they're living according to a whole new belief system—and so they're having a whole new experience!

You can begin by simply creating a mind movie about your future self thriving on the other side of what you're releasing. This is very similar to what we discussed in chapter 2, but with one difference: this time we're going to hang out with our future selves. So, if you're working through a love block, you can see your future self absolutely thriving with a future partner in a happy, healthy relationship. If you're working through a money block, you can see your future self making more money than ever and managing it with so much peace. And so on. In this visualization, imagine that your future self can grant you wisdom. They know something that you don't yet. Present them with your current concern and hear what they'd say. Let them show you how good it gets.

When we do this, it helps us to get beyond the present moment and our limited scope. Inherently, we do believe in ourselves—yes, you, or else you would not be reading this book and you *certainly* would not have gotten this far into it! You believe the future holds great promise and potential for you. So lean into that. See your future self. You'll zoom out from the version of you that has it all figured out, and you'll see something different. You'll call on faith. And a message *will* come through. Perhaps sprinkled with wisdom, a next step, or at the very least . . . comfort.

Your future self is and will always be one of the greatest neural pathways you can build out. It changes your expectations completely. And from a quantum physics perspective, it's actually helping you connect with a version of you that already exists.

You, currently, are the future self of your past self. In the same way you look back on your past self and want to send them love, comfort, and perspective, your future self is doing the same with you. You can see how it all turned out for the past you who was so worried! And you know that life is a beautiful unfolding process where new characters and plot developments can pop up out of left field. Previous worries that kept you up all night dissolved into the rearview mirror as solutions miraculously appeared and things turned out better than your terrified subconscious mind could have even hoped. You actually know this series of events quite well.

In between rounds of tapping, pull up your favorite mental mind movies. Ask for wisdom. See your future self. Get a hug from them. The imagined future, when imagined enough, becomes reality.

Rewiring with Affirmations

When I began my journey with EFT, the aftercare of my brain was so important. Because this work is really belief-overhaul work, the question of "What would you rather believe?" yields the most life-changing possible answers. Because our beliefs have been encoded in our subconscious mind, they're running the show beneath the surface, unbeknownst to us. We seldom question them *until* we do this work. But once we do, strengthening their neural pathways is extremely important.

Affirmations are the way here—and not how you think. Early on in my mindset-shifting journey, I got really into affirmations for the first time. My plan was simple, and I believed it would change my entire life: on my long walks to class, I'd do nothing but mentally rehearse my affirmations over and over again. I really gave it my best, most diligent effort. But no surprise here, it got me nowhere—because I wasn't in the right brainwave state for my subconscious to receive this reprogramming attempt.

We can *actually* access our subconscious minds when our brains are in lower brainwave states. By "brainwaves," I really do mean waves: these are measured using an EEG machine, and there's a specific range for each brainwave.

Here's an overview of your brain's brainwave states:

Beta State: Right now, if you've had a big cappuccino (oh, that's me writing this) and you're reading all this information intently, you're likely in a beta brainwave state. This is the second highest one. At a frequency of 12–38 Hz, it's the brainwave state of alertness. Whenever you're solving problems, thinking actively, engaged in interesting conversation, or making a decision, you're in a beta state. This is usually the peak of your day: whenever you're focused, deliberating on mental focus, or ALL IN on what you're doing in a very active way, you're in beta.

Gamma State: The only state above beta is gamma, which is characterized by incredible concentration. This can go two ways: One is with deep spiritual introspection, such as if you're a sage meditating guru. If you can really reach deep levels of consciousness through a meditation practice, you can reach the gamma state that way. Personally, this has never happened for me. But I'll keep you posted. However, another form of gamma state that we're more aware of is incredible concentration on one thing we're doing. Think about the last time you were laser focused, locked in, whether it was a creative flow or a problem-solving task. When background sounds seem to fade out and you lose all track of time because of PEAK focus and concentration, this is the gamma state. It's anywhere from 38 to 100 Hz.

Alpha State: Below beta is alpha, which is a more relaxed state. You're still awake, but you're not quite as alert . . . your brain is just taking a breather.

Think about the last time you stared out the window daydreaming or got lost in the flow of more mindless creative work, such as coloring or playing a song on the piano you've played hundreds of times before. This isn't active creative work with your problem-solving brain (beta state). Think about a really good morning of journaling or, if you like to sing, the mode when you're feeling the rhythm and letting it move through you without much thought. Alpha state can also be reached in a light meditation, such as if you closed your eyes right now to take several deep breaths. The bonus of alpha state is how much it can assist with creativity—you've experienced this anytime you've ever been in flow, when it seems like you're channeling forth what you're creating as opposed to thinking and deliberating through every element of it. You can also visualize more vividly in this relaxed state, with stronger mental imagery. Alpha state's EEG falls between 8 and 12 Hz.

Theta State: For the sake of rewiring, this is our juicy, ideal brainwave state. Tucked right below alpha at 3.5–7.5 Hz, theta is best characterized as that funky brainwave state between relaxation and being conked out asleep. Have you ever noticed when you're falling asleep, there's a slippery slope between coherent thoughts and then half dreams that make little to no sense from a conscious perspective? One second, you're mentally thinking through what you need from the grocery store the next day as your body starts to relax more and more, and next thing you know, you have a weird half dream occurring involving a moose, an orange shade of lipstick, and your middle school English teacher. You're still technically "awake," but you're so relaxed that little is making sense.

Bingo. This is where we want to be. In this low brainwave state, your brain is wide open to suggestion. Because if your mind can spiral into silly storylines and temporarily believe they are true and happening, it can *definitely* accept a suggestion like, "I now easily and naturally run my dream business."

Remember how we talked about the Critical Faculty, or the gatekeeper of your subconscious mind earlier in this book? That gatekeeper is not on shift during this brainwave state. Your brain is simply too relaxed. I once literally saw the security guard of my apartment complex asleep on the job in the middle of the night. It's easy to slip into deep relaxation when everything is so quiet and dark and the vibes are extra sleepy, and your Critical Faculty is no exception. It's checked out.

But we love this—because we can take full advantage of it. Here's what you're going to do.

1. You're going to write down everything about the life you want. This includes your new belief systems. You're going to write it down as if it's already happened. So, if you want a promotion at work, your statement could be something like, "I'm so happy and grateful to have been promoted at work!" If you've been rewriting the belief that you'll never find love, you'd write down what you'd rather believe but take it a step further. It isn't just now believing that you WILL find love—we have to construct a statement that is active and present. In this case, it could be something like, "I feel so loved by my partner."

   Please, though, one caveat here: this cannot be a statement about what you DON'T want. Your subconscious doesn't actually hear the words "not" or "not anymore." So, if you have an affirmation like, "I'm so grateful to not be unemployed anymore," it's only hearing "unemployed." If you have an affirmation like, "I no longer feel lonely," it's only hearing *lonely*. Even if you say, "I'm so grateful to be debt-free," it is only hearing *debt*, minus the *free*! Basically, it's hearing, "I'm so grateful to still be in debt." You must write what you would rather believe, which would be *employed* instead of *unemployed*, *connected* instead of *lonely*, and *abundant* instead of debt-free as potential rewrites for the aforementioned phrases. Your subconscious is *so* literal. Be very, very careful and diligent here.

2. Get EVEN MORE specific. It's epic to have statements about meeting The One, landing the promotion, getting into that graduate program—but we also want to construct a very vivid picture of this imagined future for your subconscious to make it *extra* real. This is the really fun part. Imagine I hand you a magic wand in the form of a pen, and now you get to write exactly how you'd experience all the things you want in detail. Now, "I've met The One" becomes "I love my date nights with my partner at our favorite restaurant, we have so much fun and communicate so well together." And "I got into my dream college" becomes "I love my days on campus at (college name), studying with my friends and enjoying the (state name) sunshine."

Think about it like this: we are trying to trick your subconscious. There, I said it. We are being sneaky-sneaky. We have a plan and we're going undercover. To do this effectively, we have to convince your subconscious that this future has actually already happened and is your real reality right here, right now. If you actually got your dream job, would your only thought about it be "I'm so grateful I got my dream job"? Likely, no. Sure, there's some of that, which is why it's worth mentioning, but you'd also be feeling grateful for the day-to-day of *having* your dream job. So go into all the best parts. Create a very clear and compelling narrative of what it looks like and feels like to achieve the next level in your life.

3. Once you have written all of this down, you're going to record your own voice saying these affirmations. There are apps for this, or you can record it in your phone's voice memos or on your computer. I personally enjoy the ThinkUp app because I can put the recording of my voice on loop all night. We are doing this so that you can listen to these affirmations when you're in the theta brainwave state as you're falling asleep. You may wonder what is different about this versus any other multi-hour video or audio you could find online and press play on for all-night listening, which admittedly does sound easier. But here are the two main reasons you are best served to do it this way:

a. You can be hyperspecific to *your* vision of the future. Sure, there is a great abundance of worthiness affirmations online. But we want to really convince your subconscious that this is *real*, and this is happening now. The more specific we can be, the better. You know exactly what you want, and how you want that to play out—and even if you generally want the same thing as others, such as hitting a $1 million profit year or becoming famous, no one else's affirmations will ever be as effective as your own. Because only you want what you want in the way that *you* want it.

b. Listening to the affirmations stated in present tense in your own voice is the sneakiest rewiring trick of all. To your subconscious mind in this low brainwave state, it's being perceived as if you are actively saying it. And our Critical Faculty gatekeeper is off duty, gently snoring in dreamland. There's nothing stopping or buffering your subconscious from taking your own words on as truth. You recognize the sound of your own voice. So hearing yourself say it sounds extremely legitimate. Why would you lie? Sure, you may have a practice of stating your affirmations out loud in your waking life, but that's when your Critical Faculty is on duty. It's blocking those statements left and right, because it has no evidence to back them up. "Hm, not true," it says as it chucks your attempt to rewire your subconscious out the window. Hence, why my long walks to class with diligent affirmation reciting did nothing.

In my experience, hearing my own voice say it usually mixes in with my weird half dreams. I've had cool moments of actually feeling myself accept the programming. My brain will create a whole mental narrative to go with the affirmations, such as me actually seeing the accomplishment play out and experiencing it as real. Or one time it made up a mind movie of me telling my mom one of the affirmations as if it had already happened. Those are just the instances I remember—which is miraculous enough, since we seldom remember anything from this funky theta brainwave state. It just goes to show how much is really happening underneath the surface as we're falling asleep listening to these affirmations in our own voice.

Finally, there's a safety component here. As you know by now, your subconscious is chiefly concerned with your safety. It quite literally believes that the next level of your life is a threat to your livelihood and well-being, even though we know *consciously* that that is ridiculous, and of course it's safe. So having your subconscious hear your own voice say these affirmations as if they're true *as* you're falling asleep and deeply relaxed is extra powerful. Essentially, you're sending a brand-new message: "I have now achieved X goal, and I am completely okay." In fact, you're so okay with it that your heart rate is low and relaxed and your nervous system is regulated! It's the ultimate trick. It's utilizing your sleepy, cozy, safe theta brainwave state to plant a brand-new paradigm in your subconscious—which will always lead to rapid rewiring: yes, this is 100 percent safe, look how *calm* we are!

CHAPTER REVIEW AND EXERCISES
TL;DR

• EFT Tapping can be used to rewire our subconscious beliefs and patterns, leading to lasting change in our lives.

• We can identify a block through sights, sounds, sensations, pictures, memories.

• Clearing blocks from the root changes the brain's neural pathways. The further back we go, the more we clear. An early memory is more likely to be the root of the tree, which is more effective for rewiring than just cutting off branches of a tree.

• I strongly recommend you don't just TL;DR this tapping process, but as a review:

  • Identify the memory or belief causing the block.

  • Notice how the memory affects the body (emotionally or physically).

  • Tap on the meridian points while recalling the memory and associated feelings.

  • Repeat the process, tapping on different memories related to the belief.

  • Use pattern interrupts in between to shift energy and rewire the brain faster.

  • Create mind movies visualizing the desired belief and future.

Memory Makeover

Let's get to it. I'll emphasize here that it's incredibly important to use discernment when doing this work on your own. For memories that are distressing or traumatic in any way, PLEASE consult a one-on-one practitioner to work through them with you. We are not meant to do trauma work on our own, nor should we.

However, we can rewire "minor" memories to begin to change our belief systems. For this exercise, we'll go back to the exercise from chapter 3, when you were encouraged to choose a limiting belief and find counterevidence of it. Let's continue clearing that up, if that feels good to you! Or choose any other minor limiting belief and an accompanying memory.

Go back into the memory and tap through it. Here are some twists to help you REALLY rewire.

On the first round of tapping, stand on one foot the entire time. Yep, flamingo style. Let yourself giggle and feel silly and playful as you lose your balance at some points.

Then, close your eyes and replay the memory, but imagine that it's snowing big cotton balls in the memory, and lots of adorable bunnies are running around collecting them in baskets for the giant bunny statue in their main square. For the tail, of course. It's gotta be one big, big tail.

Go back and check it.

This time, when tapping, speak out loud about the memory and say "it's safe to let this go" . . . but in a different accent. Or a celebrity imitation. Any voice different from your "normal voice"—and one that makes you laugh.

Then, imagine that the memory can shrink down, down, down to the size of a laundry pod, and a llama grabs it from you and throws it in the washing machine, where it spins around and around, dissolving and disappearing.

One more round, let's go! This time, speak out loud what you would have rather had happen in this memory. You can also prepare by writing some affirmations about what you'd rather believe beforehand. Then, state those out loud.

For your final visual, imagine yourself moving forward from here, empowered in your new belief system and living out the life of your dreams. Play that mind movie three times, making it better and better each time. What's the best thing that gets to happen next?

Whew! Don't you feel better?!

PART 3

MAGIC
EVER AFTER

CHAPTER 8

UNSEEN MAGIC AND TRUSTING THE TIMING OF YOUR LIFE

This entire book is evidence of unseen magic and divine timing in my own story.

More than five years ago, part of the reason I felt so stuck is because I desperately wanted to get a book out there with a major publisher. So, I got to work shopping my book proposal to literary agents. I scoured the entire literary marketplace and sent off emails to every agent remotely in the self-help or wellness category. I took the time to thoroughly research the agent, find commonalities between me and them (NOT easy, because at what point do you look like a stalker when you're three years deep in their Instagram feed?), and tailor my email pitch to what I thought they'd like. On top of that, I was asking everyone and their mother if they knew any literary agent in the whole wide world and begging for email introductions (in a cool, casual, not desperate way). By all standards, it should've been a rapid success. But, alas, crickets.

Finally, one day, I got an email expressing interest back from *one* agent. And, if there was an agent to get a hit back from, it was probably this woman—she had worked for several of the top publishing houses in leadership roles and had decades of experience under her belt. "Let's jump on a call," her email said. "Although I am concerned about your social reach, this is a strong proposal." Gulp! At that time, my online audience was around 5,000 people, and top platforms like TikTok hadn't even come into my field of awareness yet.

I got on the call wide-eyed, pen in hand, ready to jot down anything she had for me, with a tiny flame of a belief that maybe, just maybe, I could convert her into believing that I really didn't need that whole social media thing in order to get a book out there.

She gave it to me straight. "This is a really strong proposal. It could be a major book for your generation," she said, sending goose bumps down my spine. I resisted squealing and held my breath, waiting for what was next.

"However, you really need to have a *much* larger audience online for a publisher to take you seriously," she said, sharing a target number that felt like a stomach punch. Welp, no danger of an excited squeal anymore! I felt like a balloon animal that just got pricked by a pin, quickly losing air and hope.

Here she was, saying this like it was no big deal. Her tone felt like she'd just said, "All ya gotta do is hit the grocery store and grab three bananas!" Were we KIDDING? She gave me a few ideas on how I might start trekking the uphill battle to that number, but I was barely listening. I was cloaked in discouragement.

I didn't know it at the time, but that day was necessary in my journey because it gave me a goalpost I wouldn't have given myself. And although I had NO idea how I was going to get from where I was to where I needed to be, I now knew where I needed to go, and that was a start.

Thank goodness I had started tapping around this time. As I worked through how hard it all felt, new ideas and resources and connections started coming to me. Notably, I was catching up with a friend from college via phone and she said, "You should start posting on TikTok! I just did and I got three hundred followers in one day from a video that did well." Ding ding ding! A light bulb.

As I've said, healing is like layers of an onion, and tugging at a ball of yarn. So, that seed of an idea was definitely clarity, but not quite enough clarity. For some reason, my brain interpreted that piece of insight as "Okay, I watch TikTok videos to laugh. So I just need to wait until something REALLY funny happens to me!"

A few weeks later, something did. I was told by friends who lived in Scottsdale that I could just go to a hotel pool nearby, that they do it "all the time." I went ahead and did so, but completely lost my cool when I was asked my last name and room number. Because I'm a goodie two-shoes and can't lie or even pull a prank without breaking out in a rash and laughing like a nervous hyena, I fled the scene—and in the parking garage walking back to the car, whipped out TikTok and filmed myself telling the story.

And that, my friends, is the story of my first viral TikTok.

How was this going to help me build a loyal audience that would ultimately bring my dreams of being an author to life? Absolutely zero idea, but it was a start—it showed me the power of TikTok, and it was incredibly exciting to see the number of views rapidly increase. It was highly satisfying.

I just kept tapping, taking it from all angles, and finally got enough clarity subconsciously to realize I should just post about the things I like talking about anyway, which at that time was along the lines of entrepreneurship and self-help. And the unfolding process began. I started finding my groove. I kept tapping. I'd get a few more views on a video here and there. I kept applying the Subconscious Breakthrough Formula—and huge shifts started to occur.

A huge part of this was in my authenticity and showing up as ME. Not waiting for a funny story to happen (especially one as OFF-BRAND as sneaking into a hotel pool!), but sharing the things I care about, think about, talk to my friends about, and obsess about. And FINALLY, I turned a corner and realized my soul really wanted me to talk about the healing work I was doing, the dreams I was chasing, and the manifestation and spirituality principles that were rapidly changing my life. In other words, everything you've read so far in this book. I kept applying all these principles on my journey to success. Visualization. More tapping. More

YOU HAVE THE MAGIC

subconscious detective work ... then more tapping. And I had the time of my life as I did so.

In June of 2020, I finally broke 10,000 on TikTok. I kept honing what I wanted to say. I kept leaning into the fun. By September of 2020, I hit 100,000. Two months later in November, I hit 200,000.

I'd done it. And the wild part of all of it was that in the journey, I completely ... forgot about my book. That feels wild to write IN my book, but I say it for a very important reason.

So often, with this whole timing thing, we are constantly measuring ourselves by how far we are from our goals. We don't *mean* to—it just feels like what we want is out there in the distance, and we want to understand how we're pacing toward it. But pursuing our big dreams and goals isn't like running a marathon, where we know it's exactly 26.2 miles, and we know on mile 7 that there are 19.2 miles to go. It's more ambiguous than that. I didn't know I was getting closer on the day I had the conversation with the literary agent. I didn't know I was getting closer when I decided to take the advice of sneaking into that pool. There's no way I could've seen any of that.

But what it led to was a journey and adventure that has been so deeply, profoundly FUN. I had no idea the joy that was waiting for me as I started to create content. It brought me back home to myself, because I'd always wanted to be on camera. It helped me bring my talk show superstar dreams to life! And it helped me connect with hundreds of thousands of other humans who believe in the same principles I do. It's even brought me to my very best friends—my two best friends found me on TikTok!

I'm glad the agent hadn't said, "Woohoo, let's go for it!" on that call. I'm glad I was challenged. I'm glad I suddenly had a long road ahead of me. Because the road doesn't feel long when it's so fun. Imagine if someone told you right now, "You have a grand adventure ahead. It's going to be a blast, more fun than you've ever had. You're going to experience so much magic, so much success, and meet your people. Oh, but there's a catch."

You'd hesitate.

Then imagine they said, "The catch is that . . . it's going to be a really *long* adventure."

What's the problem with *that*? Sure, sign me up for a really long time of fun and magic! Because that's what life is about. Here are some of my rules for understanding the timing of your life that will totally transform your perspective on where you are and where you're going.

1. Anything can change at ANY time.

This is truly one of the most exciting parts of life. As I like to say, divine timing can sometimes mean tomorrow. You could quantum leap into a new reality by next week—you never know what is going to happen, or when. Start to tell yourself the story of exactly that! What could change everything? Who could you meet? What piece of content could you create? What idea could you come up with? Life is always brimming with possibility; but as we've talked about thoroughly in this book, we'll miss it unless we are looking for it and thinking about it.

The other part of this is an observation of mine. My opinion on divine timing has changed in recent years. I've always considered myself spiritual, which means I'm heavy on surrender and full trust. While that's still true, I've seen so many incredible shifts occur from subconscious breakthroughs and tapping work that have quite literally changed the timing of someone's life (including mine). So here's what I posit: What if divine timing isn't about something being destined to happen for you on a specific day in six months or five years? What if divine timing means YOU become aware of your own divinity, and release and let go of any blocks in the way of receiving and experiencing it Right Now or at a time that better serves you?

This is where we talk about speeding up the timeline of events. I genuinely believe that whatever timeline you have in your head for a goal can be dramatically reduced by looking within and understanding your own subconscious blocks to its rapid manifestation. WHY would your subconscious want you to take your sweet time? Is it possible that you're just not ready?

Which brings me back to how this book is evidence of divine timing. I see now incredibly clearly how, when I first started reaching out to agents, I was not at *all* subconsciously ready to write an entire book about any of this. I was not subconsciously ready to have a big book deal, to work with a publisher, to put my book out into the world. I had so many fears about how I was perceived. I had concerns about whether I was smart enough or talented enough. I consciously wanted it so, so badly, but my subconscious was sounding off alarms left and right whenever I tried to pursue it.

I know my subconscious put up a fight, because I look back and see with perfect clarity how the answers were all around me, and all I had to do was follow the path. But I was misguided. I was blocked from very obvious paths and possibilities in front of me, like there were blinders in front of my eyes. I had so much to heal about my self-perception. I also had a lot to learn as I built my audience about not internalizing what others may think of me and my work. This was one of the hardest things I had to rewire and overcome—and I can't imagine being thrown to the proverbial wolves during that first year. I was not ready to be perceived, to read hate comments about myself, and to stay in a space of security and confidence. I had to work through all of that for *any* of it to feel safe to come in.

As I healed all of this, the idea for my book came back around. It started as a whisper: "Hey, remember that book?" and then an internal enthusiastic yell: "Let's do this!!!" I knew it was time. And once I knew, I went after it. Suddenly, what had been so beyond difficult beforehand was the easiest thing in the world. I didn't query a single agent—I got hit with the idea to ask someone on Instagram I'd messaged with a few times to refer me to hers, and a few quick emails later, I was introduced to my epic agent. It all came together like *click, click, click*. I was READY. And when your subconscious is truly, 100 percent ready, nothing is in the way anymore. It's law that what you want will come in rapidly in the best possible way for *you*.

So, take a moment to pause and consider: Are you *really*, 100 percent ready for what you want? Return to the subconscious breakthrough questions if necessary. And when you're done with those, I have a brand-new one for you: What is your expectation of the timeline of how this can and will come together for you?

Subconscious Breakthrough File

We often think that the big things we want aren't going to happen for a long, long time. Our brain equates "big, life-changing moment" with a future date, *far* in the future, after everything has changed. But this isn't necessarily true, and believing it can drain us of our faith and power in this moment, similar to the belief that we need something outside of us to come in and change our lives. It keeps us in "waiting energy"—that sticky place where we feel like we're sitting around anticipating that something will come true. We've all been there; and not just at the DMV. If you've ever been awaiting big news about a job application or college acceptance and refreshed your email at least one hundred times in a one-hour span, you know that Waiting Energy feeling. This drains a lot of our present power, because we aren't present in *this* moment—we're waiting for something outside of us to make us feel better.

It reminds me of one of my clients and friends, Ashley, who had a belief from a very young age that the only path forward toward her financial dreams was to win the lottery.

"I had a belief that in order to achieve my goals I had to win the lottery," she reflected. "I used to play the lottery every chance I could. I didn't believe I could achieve my goals without external financial aid. Working with Haley with EFT Tapping helped shift this belief that I needed extra financial support to believing I was capable of achieving my goals by *just being me*. I needed to heal the beliefs that I wasn't enough or worthy of being the person who could achieve her goals on her own."

The passive nature of this goal—one that kept her waiting and wishing by continuously playing the lottery—had Ashley's entire life in limbo. Until she started tapping and applying the work we've talked about in this book.

"I thought I was destined to live a life on autopilot, work, come home, eat dinner, and watch a show each night. Go on a few vacations each year and repeat. It wasn't until I worked with Haley that I felt I could change my life through EFT Tapping. I no longer felt trapped. Since EFT Tapping my life has transformed. The belief in myself and my abilities have skyrocketed. . . . Haley and EFT Tapping have given me a life I don't need a vacation from."

At the time of writing this, Ashley just hit $1 million in revenue from her business. She released the belief it had to be hard. She released the belief that she needed a future event of winning the lottery to set her free financially. When she released the waiting and turned within, she used her genius and resources to build a business where she's thriving, really helping others, and making a consistent income that allows her to live the life of her dreams!

The old belief may have been "In divine timing, I'll win the lottery."

Now, the truth floods in: "I go within, understand my blocks and limiting beliefs, and I release them. I make my own divine timing, while trusting that the Divine has beautiful surprises in store on the journey."

2. It all makes sense when you arrive.

I'll lean back on my quote about divine timing for this point, and because it's worth mentioning again: "I go within, understand my blocks and limiting beliefs, and I release them. I make my own divine timing, while *trusting that the Divine has beautiful surprises in store on the journey.*"

In my own journey to this book, the timing was up to my subconscious—but the journey had an air of divinity to it that I never could have seen at the time. The beauty of life is knowing you're going to arrive at the goal, or at the mountaintop, and when you do, it will all make sense. You'll see with perfect clarity what you had to learn to get there. You'll see where the journey led you, and what it brought to you. What I wanted desperately at that moment redirected me onto a profound healing journey to completely transform my subconscious and my career. It led me to start offering EFT Tapping and subconscious breakthroughs via my Dreamaway membership community. And so many beautiful events unfolded like I was following breadcrumbs.

Notably, I hosted a giveaway for a one-on-one coaching call, back when I was first getting started. Of the hundreds of people who entered, I randomly chose one girl. She was wearing a hat and sunglasses in her profile picture, so I didn't even know what she looked like, and her handle was a nickname, not even her real name.

That girl ended up becoming my very best friend, Ankita. What's even more wild? She KNEW we were destined to be best friends just from seeing my content online. She felt it intuitively.

My other best friend, Lyss, saw my content online as well, and ALSO had an intuitive nudge that we would be best friends. She slid into my DMs a few years ago, we got dinner, and we have been inseparable ever since.

I've met so many remarkable people in my career so far. And it all started with pursuing this abstract goal a literary agent told me once. While I'm thrilled I am finally bringing this book into the world, I have to say that thrill quite literally multiplies when I reflect on the entire series of events that led me here.

Which leads me to something really beautiful I believe about divine timing. Remember, your goal isn't predestined and written in the stars to happen on a very specific autumn Tuesday in a couple of years. Instead, the sequence of events *gives* the ultimate event its meaning, just like words in a sentence.

Take these two sentences.

"I saw a moose with binoculars."

"With binoculars, I saw a moose."

They're exactly the same words, no additions or subtractions. However, the two sentences have slightly different meanings because of the sequence of the words. The first sentence is unclear—one reading could imply that the moose had binoculars, which is adorable. But the second sentence makes more rational sense: it means I saw a moose through my binoculars.

The same is true of events. Think about one of those great romance movies where the two main characters turn from enemies to lovers. Imagine that there are two key scenes:

- The one where one character accidentally spills red wine on the other's white dress and they share harsh words and stomp off in opposite directions.

- The one where they lock eyes at a concert and share their first kiss.

If this happened in order of how I wrote them, it would be a classic chick flick. They can't stand each other, then ultimately fall in love.

But imagine if the sequence was reversed, and the kiss happened first, and the dramatic red wine scene happened later. The meaning of the story would be completely different. It's no longer an enemies-to-lovers tale; it's a lovers-to-enemies tale. Very, very different stories.

The same is true of your life. The order in which things happen determines what happens next and changes the story. I want you to start seeing this as something that's always working in your favor. Assume the best, always: if it's not here yet, and you are diligently clearing any subconscious blocks, it's because a few other things need to happen first to make it as great as it can possibly be. It always makes sense in time. You will realize why it couldn't have happened a second sooner, thanks to all the things that happened before—which, by the way, could include the identification and rewiring of subconscious blocks.

I genuinely believe that having a desire, dream, or goal sparks a journey within itself. One of my favorite quotes is by Supreme Court Justice Sonia Sotomayor: "But experience has taught me that you cannot value dreams according to the odds of their coming true. *Their real value is in stirring within us the will to aspire.* That will, wherever it finally leads, does at least move you forward."

Deciding to pursue what you want—no matter what it is, whether you dream of seeing your name in lights or you want to meet your person—will lead you on a journey within. Any limiting belief or block that comes up around this dream needed to be cleared in the first place to return you to the Truth of your being: that you are innately worthy, you're a powerful creator, and you're destined for every vision you have. And there are more benefits to that clearing than what meets the eye; you're never just removing a block or subconscious belief as a means to one end. It will serve you immeasurably in every possible way, opening up an entirely new world to you.

3. The purpose of your life is evolution and fun.

After all, don't you want to look back and think the same about your own journey? I have learned something beautiful about divine timing that I always want to apply to my current journeys and ambitions. It's all supposed to be fun. If we can know and feel that it's all going to ultimately make sense, what if we can see life as the pursuit of beautiful little breadcrumbs, all leading us somewhere extra beautiful?

This perspective gives us an extra dose of patience, which I've learned also gives us an extra dose of magic. There's potency in *fun*. I have experimented with many ways of working over the years, and I've noticed something that's great news for us all: the more fun you can have as you're creating or pursuing something, the better it will perform when you release it into the world. Because the trick is not to create or do things as a means to an end, but rather as an end within itself. Let this question guide you: "If nothing came from this, would I still enjoy it? Would it still be fun?"

This is a difficult question to ask yourself when you have big goals. A lot of times, we do things to get us to where we want to go. I'm not saying to throw that out—but what if every step you took toward that goal could be tripled in efficiency with a little extra FUN? What if it could be easier?

Believing in divine timing can also mean we aren't in a rush.

Unseen Magic

Another big part of faith is trusting in what is unseen. There is so much that is happening around us, behind the scenes, at any given moment of our lives—and we never know what it is until later! One of my favorite concepts to trust in—especially when I'm feeling stagnant or like there's scant evidence of progress—is "unseen magic."

You've had it too, many times, in your life—and always will! Think of unseen magic as the invisible forces of destiny that are working on your behalf. For example, you could think you're having an average day and nothing is going right in your dating life, but that's the exact day that your soulmate has decided to move to your city, which will trigger the dominoes series of events that lead to you meeting and beginning an amazing life of partnership together.

Right now, someone could be mentioning your name to someone else for a career opportunity. Or your future dream home is being built. Someone is making a strategic decision at work that will lead the way for your promotion, or your plane gets delayed and it seems like a big inconvenience, yet that's why you strike up a conversation with the person next to you at the airport coffee shop and make a new dear friend. Someone just found a video you posted and thinks you're perfect for a massive opportunity and they're about to reach out.

The belief in unseen magic is the knowing that everything is working on your behalf all the time, even when you don't see it. We'll experience many "aha!" moments long after the fact, realizing something was coming together all along. And there's much unseen magic we will never know about, that remains unseen—like why that restaurant was closed and so you went to another one, or why that road was blocked off so you had to take a different route. Magic can also mean protection, and believing you are being guided constantly. Because you ARE! And the more you tune into your own magic, the more synchronicities and magical events will seem to unfold before you and around you. It's happening RIGHT now, as you read this!

CHAPTER REVIEW AND EXERCISES
TL;DR

• We can and should address subconscious blocks that may be causing delays and obstacles. But the entire process serves us, delays included. Sometimes a greater story is unfolding out of all of it.

- The "long road" is an adventure filled with unexpected magic, growth, and connection. The journey itself can be fulfilling and transformative, even if the outcome is not immediately apparent.

- Part of divine timing is the divine series of events. Some things have to happen first, and you'll be so grateful for that when you arrive! Surrender the order and keep showing up with your most heartfelt intention.

- So much is working on your behalf behind the scenes. Trust in unseen magic, even when it is, true to name, "unseen."

When the Unseen Became Seen

To prove to yourself the power of unseen magic, review your own life to date. What happened in the perfect way at the perfect time, even though it didn't seem like it in the lead up?

You can also answer this question by revisiting past delays and obstacles that ended up working out perfectly. What greater story was being woven through it all?

Based on what you can see now, write a letter to your past self reassuring them that it's all working out perfectly. What do you wish they knew?

And here's a twist: whatever you write to your past self has breadcrumbs of what your future self would want to tell you, right now.

CHAPTER 9

DAILY ROUTINE FOR MAGIC

Ａs you continue to step into the magic of your life, please remember: you will continue to be the alchemist of your life experience. This means that the magic you create will grow and grow with your time, energy, and attention to it—and, although it's always within you, it can wane and become dormant if you aren't aware of it. This is, admittedly, one of the hardest things to remember and put into practice. My entire career is about this work, and even I sometimes forget the power of mindset work, vibration, and meditation—but life keeps guiding me back, because it works every time!

What helps me most is staying on top of my EFT Tapping practice. There are times I'll feel better than ever in my mindset, then something will happen that will feel discouraging or trigger a past limiting belief. When this happens, I don't suppress it or say, "Oh, I already tapped on or worked through something adjacent to this, so this is fine." I make sure to sit with the feeling, understand its roots, understand what my subconscious is trying to tell me, and work through it—or else it can derail me. I don't say this to scare you, but to keep you aware. When your experience shifts, keep leaning into those shifts and thickening those neural pathways by envisioning the new. Tap through any miscellaneous beliefs or feelings that may come up from new angles, even if this is just a quick round of tapping in the morning after you awake from a funky dream. Rome wasn't built in a day. This work is truly about consistency and staying in self-partnership to notice, as you move through your life, where energy feels sticky and how you can clear what comes up. Remember that healing is never a race. You'll never be "done" healing. Life is here for your enjoyment, evolution, fulfillment, and learning—and these are tools that will help you make the most of that and create a life around you that looks more like your internal vision.

These daily practices will help you immensely when you need a pick-me-up. They'll help you remember your magic and stay in touch with it energetically.

Today's Magic Moments

This first exercise is so fun as a journaling prompt, or as a mental exercise as you're falling asleep at night.

In any given day, we have so many magical things happen that we didn't expect. Sure, the average day likely doesn't have a life-defining win, but there are still so many pockets of joy. Think back through your day and really let yourself savor the best parts. Here are some ideas on what these magic moments can be—and notice in these examples just how "small" yet meaningful they are:

- A really delicious cup of coffee
- A funny text from a friend that made you giggle
- A productive hour of work sitting in the sunshine
- A fun time cooking and listening to your favorite album
- Great feedback from your boss
- A heart-to-heart conversation with your partner
- Making fun plans for the weekend or the summer
- Loving your outfit or lipstick shade
- A vibe change in the air, like it beginning to feel like fall
- Watching an interesting and entertaining show or movie
- Finding an amazing new song
- Getting to sleep in an extra hour
- Having an especially good lunch

I really do find that they're moments I don't expect; even on busy or stressful days, I'll have pockets of time where I'm really in the flow, when I get to do something fun, when I have a great conversation with a friend, and I love to look back on those moments in appreciation. This is a great way to flex that gratitude and appreciation muscle, which primes your brain to look for *more* magic in the next day. Remember, your subconscious mind is usually looking for risks or things to worry about and complain about. This will completely change the energy winds of your life because you're training your brain to look for the positive, which goes against the grain of its natural motivations. But, as you'll see, it makes all the difference.

Evidence of Guidance

Similarly, we also have so many things happen in an average month that prove we are always being guided and things are always working out for us. One that immediately comes to mind is a time that I was stressed about making it to my next meeting in time as I was in the elevator leaving my previous appointment. The elevator stopped on another floor, and I suppressed the desire to roll my eyes, anxious to get where I was going. A man came into the elevator, checked his watch, and said, "Ah! Right on time."

I felt at that moment that it was a sign for me; not just about making my next meeting on time (which I did despite the drama), but cluing me in that I was right on time in my life in general. We all are, always, even when it doesn't feel like it. But this little moment gave me exactly what I needed.

Whenever something happens or is said around you that feels like a sign—let it be a sign! This could be as simple as a time I ordered lunch and it arrived the exact second my virtual meeting ended. I thought to myself, "perfect timing!" and it truly was—evidence that perfect timing is happening all around me in big and small ways!

With this perspective, life becomes infinitely more magical because we're looking for the proof that everything is happening for us, not to us. Survey your own life and find symbolic examples of this. Another for me: when I was apartment hunting in New York City years ago, I really had my eye on one building, but they couldn't get me in for a single apartment viewing in the entire two-day span I was visiting the city. I saved some time at the end of my second day to call again as a last-ditch effort, and when I called, it was yet again a no.

With that free time in my schedule, I went rogue and decided to, "just for fun," check out a building that was out of my price range. They got me in to view apartments *immediately*, and somehow, the price per studio apartment was significantly lower than I'd been quoted in my initial email inquiries. As I toured the unit and the building, I felt a growing sense of excitement in my heart space. It didn't only feel right—it felt expansive and exciting. And I was going to get my first two months free!

I ended up signing a lease that afternoon at that building, and I've lived in the same building ever since at the time of writing this. If the other building had been able to get me in, I wouldn't have toured my dream building, which has been a wonderful home for me.

To make matters even more exciting, my check number for the apartment's deposit happened to be #1111, and the lease was emailed to me at 11:11 a.m. for signing. These were just extra little "winks" to prove I was on the right track. And finally, when I was making the flight to New York City on my moving day, I weighed my luggage before checking it. It was stuffed to the brim with everything I could fit, and my suspicion that it was probably overweight was confirmed on the scale—55.5 pounds. But I was too excited by that little Universe wink of the repeating number "555" to be upset about the fee for the extra weight!

I brought my bag to the counter to check it, and the agent put it on the scale. I winced, knowing she was about to see that it was 5.5 pounds overweight. But as we both looked at the scale, my jaw dropped:

The scale showed exactly 50.0 pounds. EXACTLY. I wasn't charged for anything, and I knew the entire experience was another wink from the Universe! At the time, I had been feeling very anxious about my move—this was the exact sign I needed.

I keep all these little experiences in a note in my phone called my "Faith Doc." Every time something happens that is faith affirming like this, I write it down. And then, whenever I'm feeling low on faith, I survey all these beautiful little cosmic winks that have happened and I immediately feel more supported.

Here are some questions to get *your* Faith Doc going:

- When is the last time you got a clear sign from the Universe/a higher power that sent a chill down your spine? This could be a little cosmic wink, or a time you asked deliberately for a specific sign and got it.

- When in the past did you feel like you were getting rejected or encountering a roadblock, but you see clearly now that it was a powerful redirection? What past rejections are you thankful for as a result?

- Is there a time in the past that you prayed for something or visualized something and it came through for you in a beautiful way?

- What experiences have you had where you now clearly see that you were being protected by something?

- Who are the most divine people in your life, and how did the Universe guide you to them, or them to you?

• What parts of your life were totally unexpected, but ended up being your greatest blessing (e.g., your current job, the school you went to, your home, a group of friends, your running group)?

Journaling on these questions can help to jog your brain and your memory, and I strongly encourage you to continue to write them down as they come to mind—and as they occur! What I've found is the more I've leaned into these magic rituals, the more experiences of synchronicities and faith have happened. I'm excited for you to experience the same.

Daily Gratitude and Manifesting Statements

Something I started doing in the early days of my manifestation journaling was daily statements of gratitude and manifestation. I would specifically do this with my morning coffee, and I found that it really helped me center my day in where I was, what was going well, and where I was going. This sounds silly, but it's just so true—when we aren't actively thinking about our goals and ideal manifestations on a daily basis, we can lose sight of them! We always get more of what we focus on; centering ourselves in alignment with the "bull's-eye" of exactly where we want to go and what we want to experience is so powerful.

Here's how to do it. Find your new favorite journal that you can designate as your journal for this and only this. I found a mini-size one, about a quarter the size of a normal journal, because that's really all you need— one mini page per day.

Every day, you'll fill out your daily page like so:

• Add the date, with the year. You want to remember this day.

• Write down four things you're currently grateful for, using this structure: "I am so grateful for a great dinner last night with my best friend." "I am so grateful for my cozy bed." "I am so grateful for my fun plans this weekend." "I am grateful for the warm rays of sun shining through my window right now."

My "challenge" for you is to switch it up daily. It's so easy to just become robotic with this: "I'm grateful for my friends. I'm grateful for my family. I'm grateful for my job." Try to never write the same statement twice, unless it's super relevant. I like to go into details: which friend am I extra grateful for today, and why? Then, "I'm so grateful for my friends" becomes "I'm so grateful for Ankita and how she always knows exactly what to say when I need encouragement." The difference is palpable.

I encourage you to look for details to incorporate into your gratitude statements. If you're grateful for your home, why? Nothing is too small. It could be your pillow being the perfect firmness or really loving the process of making your go-to breakfast. It could be how good a warm shower feels or how much you love your view of your backyard. Those details make it all even more exciting to write down, and to reflect on! Here's a hack: If you were to completely lose your memory about this stage of your life, what would you want to remember? How boring would it be to reflect and just read that you were grateful for your friends? Give your future self something so juicy to reflect on—and give your present self the opportunity to go deeper into gratitude than ever before.

Then, it's time for your manifestation statements. I want you to write these in the same format you just wrote your gratitude statements. This means you're writing them in the present tense. So, if you're manifesting your dream home, you would say, "I am so grateful to be living in my dream home." Write it as if it's a present reality. This is a fun and sneaky way to continue convincing your subconscious that your dream life *is* your present life—you just wrote down three gratitude statements about your life currently, and now you're following that same structure to write about the life you envision. But don't stop there. In the same way we want the details for the gratitude statements, we want them for the manifesting statements, too.

In the same way I encouraged you to see and feel clear details in chapter 2, do the same for your manifesting statements. Here are some examples on how this could look.

Instead of: I am so grateful to be living in my dream home.
Try: I am so grateful to be making pumpkin chocolate chip waffles in my new home's spacious white marble kitchen with the sun streaming through the big windows.

Instead of: I am so grateful I got my promotion.
Try: I am so grateful to be thriving at work with more responsibility and celebrating my promotion with my friends and coworkers.

Instead of: I am so grateful to be going to Greece this summer.
Try: I am so grateful to be watching the sun set over Santorini with an Aperol spritz in one hand and my partner's hand in the other.

Instead of: I am so grateful my partner proposed.
Try: I am so grateful to be having the time of my life planning my wedding with my partner on our Sunday afternoon date and sampling wedding cakes.

Do you see how the extra details breathe life into the statements? The extra level of detail also extends into extra excitement. These details feel tangible—like you're *really* right there. Let yourself lean into how good it could feel, and why. That's the best part!

As you continue implementing this as a daily practice, you'll also have a great little journal to look back on. One of my most inspiring life moments (that I've added to my Faith Doc!) was finding my first ever little Gratitude and Manifestation journal when I was cleaning out my desk. It was just from a few years prior, but so many of the statements had come to fruition! I remembered how impossible those goals had felt at the time, but there I was, the future self to my past self, finding the words I wrote on the other side of achieving the manifestations. That was a pretty cool feeling—and it makes me think about my future self finding my current journal, filled with my musings and hopes for the future, smiling with a knowingness that what I wanted came together in the most beautiful way. See your own future self looking back on your words, beaming with pride and gratitude. Your manifesting statements *will* become your gratitude statements; it's just a matter of time and subconscious rewiring! Trust the process of your life!

Vision Boards and Encouragement Boards

You've likely heard of vision boards, but I cannot overstate their effectiveness. A vision board is a collection of images of things and experiences you want that really excite you. This can be done with a poster board and some magazine images, but I personally love utilizing technology to make a virtual vision board that you can make your phone wallpaper.

Here's why it's important: In your brain, you have what are called "mirror neurons." You know how when you watch a movie or a show, you consciously know you're just watching television and it's not your actual reality, but when you become immersed in what's happening, it's almost as if you are there? Sometimes I crack myself up realizing I'm having thoughts about a set or a character as if I'm there in real life! This is because what's projected in front of our brains can be taken on as an experience. Think about the last time someone showed you a photo or video from their vacation. Couldn't you picture yourself there, seeing what they saw?

Mirror neurons are like little brain cells that fire not just when you perform an action, but also when you observe someone else performing that same action. They essentially mirror the behavior of others in our own brains. So, watching someone swing a tennis racket actually fires off the same way in our brains as it would if we ourselves were swinging that tennis racket.

When you create a vision board and place it where you can see it often, your brain starts to register those images and symbols as if you're already experiencing them. Your mirror neurons fire, essentially tricking your brain into believing that you are already living the reality depicted on your vision board.

This process can be powerful because your brain doesn't distinguish between what's real and what's imagined in this context. So, when you consistently expose yourself to the images and symbols on your vision board, your brain starts to align your thoughts, feelings, and actions with these images as if they're actually happening.

My phone wallpaper is a vision board of images of the life that I want to live. I strongly recommend making your phone wallpaper your own vision board, too, because every time you glance at it—whether to check for a text or to see what time it is—your subconscious is getting a flash of your dream life. Remember, we are rewiring the subconscious mind. You don't need to sit and stare at your vision board, thinking consciously about the images on it, in order to enact changes. That's what visualization is for, and it's worth a revisit to the chapter on visualization as you're building out your daily routine for magic.

RULES OF THUMB FOR MAKING A MAGICAL VISION BOARD

Look for Images That Make You FEEL Excited!

So, you know cerebrally what you WANT for your life. If I told you to list it out, you could, right here right now—especially if you got a head start on your daily manifesting statements or affirmations. The visual is a very different experience, even if you used powerful descriptive words in your statements. Search online for images related to what it is that you want. You'll find a bounty of options, and what's important is picking the ones that elicit that emotional response. Sometimes, you'll stumble across an image that's unlike anything you knew you wanted, but you'll feel that visceral reaction. I've had this happen many times with pictures of homes, vacation spots, the interior of a recording studio, you name it.

For example: If you want to manifest a trip to Paris and see the Eiffel Tower twinkle at night, search for those key words, but notice the difference in how every image makes you feel. There will be images of different views: from the Seine River, from a rooftop, from a restaurant, from a hotel, or directly beneath the Eiffel Tower. There's no right or wrong answer here on which perspective to choose; it's about *your* experience of the image. This is also how we can fine-tune what it is that we want. I think it's so fun to search for an abstract idea of something we want, and then find specifics as we go. Maybe you'll find an image you really love of the Eiffel Tower from a specific view, and you'll do some research and find out that picture was taken from a very specific restaurant or hotel. Voilà! Now you have more inspiration for your Paris trip.

This is also fun because it reminds me of childlike play. Remember when you'd let your imagination run wild, daydreaming about the future? Do this here! Give yourself full permission to want the things and experiences you want and bring them to life in Technicolor by finding images that very specifically capture the vibe and energy of what it is you want.

Remember Your MIRROR NEURONS!

There is a hack for making vision boards extra effective. Here's a common mistake: You want a cherry-red convertible. So you find an image of just that, but it's a stock image of the exterior of the car, or a cute picture of the car driving along the road. The photographer of the image took the photo of it from behind the car, or down the road from the car, or it was the car dealership's photographer. "Lookie here!" you might think. "It's the EXACT red convertible I want!"

Amazing. But we aren't just finding a picture of the specific. We need to find a picture that tricks your brain into having an *experience*. You could find the cutest aesthetic photo of that red convertible of your dreams meandering through the coastal hills of Laguna Beach, but here's my question for you: If you were the proud owner and operator of that red convertible, would *that* be your experience of being the owner and operator of the car?

No. If you own and operate a vehicle, you are the one driving it. Which means your most frequent view of the car is *not* of the exterior, even if you've found the cutest picture in the world. Your most frequent view is from the driver's seat. Or maybe you do see the car's exterior, but it's in a parking lot or a driveway as if you're walking up to it about to reach for the door handle.

I've found many great photos of boats . . . taken from a drone above. Or a couple laughing and toasting champagne on vacation . . . but how is seeing *another* couple remotely similar to the experience of *being* in that couple and cheersing your soulmate? This is what distinguishes "this is what I want" vision boards from "this is actively rewiring my subconscious to actually get everything I want" vision boards.

For everything you want, ask yourself this question: If this was my actual experience, what would I be seeing out of my own eyes? We can go back to your manifesting statements on this one, or the two can play off each other.

You may run into difficulties with this part if you want a job at a specific company and can't envision what the inside of the office looks like, for example. What you can do instead is find any image related to work that makes you feel something viscerally. Maybe it's a cute cappuccino next to a floral notebook and gel pen, which makes you think of your best flow days, when you're coming up with ideas for the week's client presentations. Use that. Then, we can refine the interpretation of the image in your brain's processing by adding an affirmation with it.

With this cappuccino and floral notebook image, you could add an affirmation like, "I'm so in the flow with work, I love brainstorming and preparing for the work week." Voilà. If there's a specific company you want to work for, go ahead and add that specific—"I'm so in the flow with my job at (Insert Company Name Here)..."

Another way to think about this assignment is: If you could call up your future self, who is living everything you've ever wanted, and ask for them to send you some images from their life that they snapped on their own, what would those images be? The more natural this seems, the better. We're fortunate to live in an age of advanced technology when making these vision boards because, guess what? Someone out there is living part of your dream life. They're living in your dream home. They have your dream job. They're going on your dream vacations. They have your dream dog or cat or bird. And they have taken images of their day-to-day experience, and those photos are now on the internet.

The Power of Photoshop

We can get extra wild with this when there are specific things we want. It's easier than ever to do our own Photoshop job, so here are some ideas for you...

1. **Photoshop Your Bank Account.** Say you're actively manifesting an extra $10,000 in your savings account. If you were to call up

your future self and ask for a picture of this, they'd likely send you a screenshot of their bank account on their phone. This is where we can get sneaky. With an application like Photoshop or Canva, you can tweak your own screenshot, so make it look exactly like it does when you log in to your current banking account—but the number will be different. As if someone waved a magic wand and your savings magically grew by $10,000, or fill-in-your-dream-number-here. You can do the same for your investment portfolios, or any app you use to survey and manage your money.

2. **Photoshop Your Sales Dashboard.** If you're an entrepreneur, there's likely one main spot where you can survey your recent sales. Use this! You can screenshot it, then edit in the ideal sales numbers you'd want. Same if you have a performance-based job at work. Start to apply a discerning eye: wherever you look to track progress or success, whether it's financial or otherwise, consider screenshotting and editing for your vision board.

3. **Photoshop Your Social Media Following.** Many of my clients are hoping to grow their personal or business accounts. This is very easy. Screenshot your profile, then think of another account that has the number of followers you'd like to manifest. You can then screenshot their account, crop the image of their followers number, and layer it on top of your profile. Note: Make sure that if you change your profile picture or handle in the future, you update this image in your vision board, too.

4. **Photoshop an Offer Letter or Acceptance Letter.** Maybe you're hoping to get into a certain graduate program or land your dream job. I've seen people photoshop this. You can see what you can find online by searching key words "X Company offer letter" or "X School acceptance letter," then once again use your handy Photoshop tools to edit in YOUR name and the date you'd like to receive the letter. Just the first part of it, such as "Your Name, Congratulations! We are pleased to offer acceptance," can work on the vision board. Don't forget the company or school logo!

5. **Photoshop a Magazine Cover.** I've also seen ultra-ambitious individuals photoshop their faces onto magazine covers—business magazines for entrepreneurs, style magazines for models. It's a cool way to know what it would look like and feel like to dominate your industry and be on the front cover of magazines across the country. Talk about a boost in motivation and confidence!

Affirmations and Lifestyle Images

I love decorating my vision board with affirmations. You'll quickly become an affirmations machine with your daily manifesting statements, so remember you can always add new ones or switch them out. This isn't required, but I do notice that when I glance at my vision board, I actually do read the affirmations as a thought. You can keep this ultra simple, like, "I am the happiest I've ever been." Or, "I am having so much fun with work lately!" Or, "I am in the flow of abundance."

As aforementioned, you can use this to add detail to images. You can include an affirmation about how easy it was to manifest something, like a picture of your dream engagement ring and an affirmation that says, "My soulmate easily and naturally glided into my life right on time." Or a picture of your dream home with an affirmation like, "I'm so excited that purchasing my dream home went so smoothly."

Remember, the words you use are very important. Sometimes it's alluring to say something like, "I can't believe how well things are going!" Well, now you have the word "can't" on your vision board, nestled right next to all those images of what you DO want.

When in doubt, really survey the words that are used. If you can be clear and direct about what exactly you *do* want, you're all set. In the same way we prune the old neural pathways of what we don't want in EFT Tapping in order to build our new neural pathways of what we do want, we must release any emphasis on what we don't want and instead solely focus on what we're calling in.

You can also utilize a vision board to emphasize the lifestyle you want to step into. For example, a few years ago I got really into health and fitness and started training for my first 5K. I wanted to stay in this epic frame of mind, so I found images of running paths and runners that made me feel excited to keep up this new lifestyle. Because that was very connected to health for me, I also found aesthetic pictures of clear glass water bottles with sliced lemons and a big bowl of berries. You wouldn't think to have that on your vision board, but it signaled to my brain a reminder of how I wanted to show up every day.

You can do the same with any habit you want to integrate or continue. If your goal is to visualize every single day, you can find an image that makes you feel excited for daily meditation, like a meditation mat or even a picture of someone meditating at sunrise. Add in the affirmation of the behavior: "It feels so fulfilling and empowering to visualize my dream life for twenty minutes every day."

In the same way that perusing vision board images can help you refine your desires, perusing habit-based images can help you tap into what would help you most right now. Recently, a big goal of mine was to have more time for writing daily. I stumbled across an image of a laptop on a tiny little corner table, like a cute writer's nook. Bingo! I actually went out and found a little corner table just like that and made my own cozy writer's nook in the corner of my home! The table is just big enough for my laptop, and it brings my vision to life.

Let Go of the How

Remember, your vision board is a construction of images of the life you are calling in. It's easy to start to consciously deliberate on how you're going to get there. We learned from a young age that when you have a goal, you must chart out a clear path for achieving it. But this can feel discouraging and overwhelming when you have a goal that feels much bigger than you, bordering on impossible at this moment in time. You MUST trust in your magic. It's not your job to figure out the How; it's just your job to believe that what you want is inevitable.

For example, when I made my first vision board, I was a college student with a very limited bank account. I wanted to go to Paris, and so I covered my vision board with images of the Eiffel Tower. I mentally resigned myself to the idea that this was a goal for the distant future, for "one day when I make enough money to go for it." But it was the most pronounced part of my vision board, and I saw it every time I looked at my phone.

Interestingly, I soon got involved in a sales competition among college students and was awarded a lump-sum bonus for being a top performer. It was the *exact* amount of money necessary to purchase plane tickets to Paris for me and my boyfriend for winter break. This came together in a matter of months in a way I never could've foreseen! I could have spent time and energy stressing about how I was going to call in the money necessary to get to Paris, which genuinely felt so impossible. Instead, I just let my subconscious take care of it. I acted when the opportunity arose and gave my all, but I never saw it coming. I still look back and scratch my head at how such a lucrative opportunity found me in college.

It reminds me of how one of my clients made a vision board including a private jet after attending one of my vision board workshops. She also did not know the "how"—financially, a trip on a private jet was lightyears away from what she could make happen in that moment. She put it on there anyway, and just months later, an opportunity came up with a group of entrepreneurs she and her fiancé were a part of to share a private jet trip from Geneva to London. They got the experience at a fraction of the cost, on a much shorter timeline than she anticipated!

ENCOURAGEMENT BOARDS

Adjacent to vision boards, or something you can do to take your vision board to the next level, is the concept of an Encouragement Board. This is basically like adding a big dose of your Faith Doc to your vision board. I came up with this idea on a day when I was really struggling with self-belief with my music. I forced myself to think about all the positive things people had said to me about my voice and my songs, and all the little divine winks I'd received from the Universe on my journey thus far. I then went through my phone and found related pictures and screenshots of this direct encouragement! I also remembered encouraging words that others had said out loud to me and wrote those down on the encouragement board, too.

This is a great way of balancing what you're calling in with the evidence you already have. This could be anything: images of what you currently have that you're really grateful for, like a certain relationship or your home. You could also add in images of things you've already manifested! The combination of your future desires and current proof infuses the entire board with a little more certainty.

If you don't feel like you have enough encouragement for this yet, don't worry. Encouragement will start coming in. Keep your eyes wide open for evidence. If you ask for a sign of a giraffe if you're going to get your dream job, and then you see a stuffed animal giraffe on the floor of the grocery store, take a picture of this! This, too, is evidence and encouragement. You can put it on your board with a note like, "A divine wink that I'm going to get my dream job!"

Remember, beliefs are games of evidence. The more you can remind yourself of your positive evidence and tell yourself the story of the life you really want to live, the more you'll see *more* evidence. And so on and so forth. Soon your board will be absolutely covered in evidence and encouragement.

EDITING AS YOU GO

We are evolving humans, and certain desires may be stronger at some times than others. You always want your board to reflect your most exciting vision for the future right now. Survey your board consciously at least once a month, and just see if anything has changed. If you are scrolling social media or flipping through a magazine and you see an image that sets your heart on fire, make a note to update your vision board by adding that image. Take things off as they no longer resonate; or update affirmations if you find better wording. You get to find clarity as you go. And, it's so fun to revisit these boards and keep refining our vision for the future!

CHAPTER REVIEW
TL;DR

• Get your RAS working for you by doing the "Today's Magic Moments" exercise (page 202), to reflect on the small, unexpected moments of joy and beauty that occur throughout the day.

• Actively look for signs and synchronicities that "wink," proving your alignment with the Universe's plan. Jot these down in a Faith Doc so you always have evidence you can reread.

• Create affirmations that read as present tense, and don't forget the details! Allow yourself to be creative with this exercise.

• Work WITH your subconscious to manifest, by listening to affirmations at night when your subconscious is most open to suggestion, and expertly selecting "POV" images for your vision board so your mirror neurons are activated.

• Relish in gratitude as much as possible, because there's so much to be grateful for on the beautiful adventure that is your life. How epic that we get to create the life of our dreams and enjoy the unfolding!

CONCLUSION

I f this book has taught you anything, I hope it's that you have the power, right now, to change your life. That's something we easily forget. Magical things happen, then the ho-hum of life as usual returns, and it's easy to lose touch with the truth that more is up to *us* than we think.

I wrote this book over the course of a year, remembering everything I wanted to write down and share from my own journey into this work. It always amazed me when I'd review the material and be reminded of a truth I needed to read in that moment, whether it was a cautionary signal that my subconscious was creating some resistance or a hug of encouragement that the divine journey is always unfolding perfectly. So my hope is that you continue to hold this book close to your heart. If you're ever feeling discouraged, ask to be guided and open this book to a random page and see what the Divine wants to say to you. Keep up your curiosity about yourself, your beliefs, and how your expectations and unconscious mechanisms are shaping your life experience.

I want you to know how powerful and magical you are. You are the magic that will make these words jump off the page and cause real shifts and changes. You are always right where you should be, profoundly loved and guided. However this book has stirred your heart or ambitions, I hope you run headlong after what you want. Keep investigating the breakthroughs. Befriend your subconscious mind. Connect with your future self. And know it's always working out for you.

There are so many times we don't get what we thought we wanted so badly, only to see later on that it was all unfolding perfectly. When the hard moments arrive, know that you're supported. I strongly recommend subconscious work on a continual basis, however it resonates—whether that's working in a one-on-one capacity with an EFT practitioner, experimenting with hypnosis, joining the Dreamaway community or another program, or maybe trying out a new subconscious rewiring modality that's been invented since the moment I wrote these words! Remembering that YOU hold the key to the breakthrough is the most important part.

There is a great path available to you that's been calling your name all along—the path to your greatest fulfillment, joy, and excitement as you follow your bliss and release all falsehoods about your identity and what can happen in your beautiful life. The TRUTH is that you are an incredible, unique, and wonderful individual with so much to offer and so much joy ahead. The best is always yet to come; your life WILL keep getting better and better, and whatever sets your heart on fire as a "YES! THAT, PLEASE!" when you close your eyes and visualize your ideal future is custom made for you. You know it! You always have.

You are the magic—not just in your own life, but for the entire world and everyone who gets to know you. I'm so excited for what's coming next for you. I have no doubt it will be nothing short of magical.

Love,

HHS

ACKNOWLEDGMENTS

This book is an amalgamation of all those who I've learned from and all who have supported me individually, as well as this project. First and foremost, thank you to my next-level, phenomenal parents, who have always wanted me to dream big for my life and helped me to believe in magic since I was young. To my mom, who guided me to EFT Tapping and has always expanded my horizons and comforted me with beautiful, divine truths. This book would never exist without her genuine desire to help me live the happiest and most fulfilled life possible—I am who I am because of her. To my dad, who is the reason I'm a writer and musician and supports all my projects and ambitions wholeheartedly.

To Tiffany Jeffers, who began as my EFT practitioner and then became everything else: my mentor, teacher, dear friend, and chosen family. Tiffany, your imprint is on everything I do. To my partner, who cried tears of happiness with me on every part of this journey and cheers me on unconditionally. Thank you for loving me so well and for being the arms I run to in every big and small milestone of this life I'm honored to get to share with you.

To Courtney Paganelli at LGR: you have been the most exceptional literary agent. Thank you for believing in me and this project and taking me on in the perfect time and in the perfect way! Adam Krasner, I feel infinitely blessed to have you as my manager, mentor, and dear friend. Shannon Kelly and the team at Running Press: thank you for seeing the magic in this book and treating it with such reverence. It's an honor to have your team as my publisher.

To all my best friends—Ankita, Lyss, Rachel, Erin, Jess, Alyssa, Victoria, Adaire—thank you for letting me go on and on about subconscious breakthroughs over dinner and texts and coffee and for embracing this work so fully, tapping with me and cheering on all my goals and ambitions. The best part is how this work also led us all to each other and how we remind each other of these truths as we do life together.

To every member of Dreamaway and every client I've had the tremendous honor of working with, thank you for inspiring me with your dedication to live the best life possible. I love laughing about cows with you, experiencing nonstop breakthroughs, and growing in community. I feel infinitely lucky and can't wait for more.

Finally, thank you to the Divine for guiding the perfect series of events. It is my prayer that this book reaches everyone who needs the words and that they feel the Divine with them as they read them. I may have written these words, but they aren't "mine," and I'm humbly grateful to be a conduit for any form of inspiration, change, hope, and comfort. It has genuinely been so much fun. Some may say it's magic!

SOURCES AND FURTHER READING

Andrade, Jorge, and David Feinstein. "Energy Psychology: Theory, Indications, and Evidence." In *Energy Psychology Interactive: Rapid Interventions for Lasting Change,* edited by David Feinstein, Fred Gallo, and Donna Eden, 199–214. Ashland, OR: Innersource, 2004.

Beecher, Henry. "The Powerful Placebo." *Journal of the American Medical Association* 159, no. 17 (1955): 1602–1606.

Church, Dawson, et al. "Clinical EFT (Emotional Freedom Techniques) Improves Multiple Physiological Markers of Health." *Journal of Evidence-Based Integrative Medicine* 24 (January–December 2019): 1–12. https://doi.org/10.1177/2515690X18823691.

Dispenza, Joe. *Becoming Supernatural: How Common People Are Doing the Uncommon.* Carlsbad, CA: Hay House, 2017.

Fox, Glenn R., Jo-Anne Bachorowski, Richard J. Powell, and Jeffrey A. Lachman. "Neural Correlates of Gratitude." *Frontiers in Psychology* 6 (2015): Article 1491. https://pubmed.ncbi.nlm.nih.gov/26483740/.

Jackowska, Marta, Fuschia Sirois, Elizabeth J. Brown, and Andrew Steptoe. "The Impact of a Brief Gratitude Intervention on Subjective Well-Being, Biology, and Sleep." *Journal of Health Psychology* 21, no. 10 (2016): 2207–2217. https://pubmed.ncbi.nlm.nih.gov/25736389/.

Maharaj, M. E. "Differential Gene Expression after Emotional Freedom Techniques (EFT) Treatment: A Novel Pilot Protocol for Salivary mRNA Assessment." *Energy Psychology: Theory, Research,* and Treatment 8, no. 1 (2016): 17–32. https://doi.org/10.9769 /EPJ.2016.8.1.MM.

Ranganathan, V. K., V. Siemionow, J. Z. Liu, V. Sahgal, and G. H. Yue. "From Mental Power to Muscle Power—Gaining Strength by Using the Mind," *Neuropsychologia* 42, no. 7 (2004): 944–956. https://doi.org/10.1016/j.neuropsychologia.2003.11.018.

Wilkes, Rick, and Cathy Vartuli. "History of Tapping (EFT)." *Thriving Now*. https://www.thrivingnow.com/history-of-tapping-eft/.